EMOTIONAL LIT...

IN THE MIDDLE SCHOOL

A 6-Step Program to Promote
Social, Emotional, and Academic Learning

Marvin Maurer, MA and Marc A. Brackett, PhD

with Francesca Plain, EdD

Foreword by Peter Salovey, PhD
Chris Argyris Professor of Psychology and Dean of Yale College
Yale University, New Haven, CT

Maurer, Marvin, 1929-
    Emotional literacy in the middle school : a 6-step
program to promote social, emotional and academic
learning / Marvin Maurer and Marc A. Brackett ; with
Francesca Plain ; foreword by Peter Salovey.
    p. cm.
    ISBN 1-887943-74-9

    1. Affective education. 2. Social learning.
3. Emotions--Study and teaching. 4. Middle school
education.   I. Brackett, Marc A. II. Plain,
Francesca. III. Title.

LB1072.M39 2004   370.15'3
                             QBI33-2063

Cover, Book Design, & Production by Andrea Cerone, National Professional Resources,
Inc., Port Chester, NY

© 2004 Marc A. Brackett & Marvin Maurer

Dude Publishing
A Division of National Professional Resources, Inc.
25 South Regent Street
Port Chester, New York 10573
Toll free: (800) 453-7461
Phone: (914) 937-8879

Visit our web site: www.NPRinc.com

Printed in the United States of America

ISBN 1-887943-74-9

Acknowledgments

Marvin would like to acknowledge his wife Phyllis and two children, Ellyn and Richard whose support was always present during the writing of this program. He would also like to thank the hundreds of middle school students who were invaluable in their contribution to the development of the program.

Marc would like to thank his family, including Horacio Marquinez, William Brackett, Jane Brackett, Steven and Leticia Nadler, and David Nadler for their support and encouragement throughout the writing of the program. The members of the Health, Emotion, and Behavior Laboratory at Yale University provided invaluable comments on numerous drafts of the program. Susan Rivers, Paulo Lopes, Daisy Grewal, Ashley Cox, Sharon Garcia, Nicole Katulak, Heidi Brooks, David Caruso, Elyse Schneiderman, and Shinzong Lee were especially helpful. Finally, comments by Zorana Ivcevic and advice from his mentors, Drs. Peter Salovey and Jack Mayer, co-founders of the ability model of emotional intelligence, were greatly appreciated.

Marvin and Marc would also like to acknowledge in loving memory, Diane Brackett, sister of Marvin and mother of Marc.

Fran would like to acknowledge her mother, Myrel, her son, Ledd Jacob, and in loving memory, her late father Alvin.

The authors would also like to express appreciation to the staff of their publisher, National Professional Resources, Inc./Dude Publishing, particularly Andrea Cerone, Dorothy Romanello, and Lisa Hanson.

Table of Contents

Foreword

When Jack Mayer and I published our first scientific article on emotional intelligence in 1990, we had no idea anyone would find this idea interesting. Essentially, we had noticed that research on human emotions was quite fragmented. Some investigators studied facial expressions, often traveling to the far reaches of the earth to interview individuals who had minimal contact with Westerners. Other investigators explored the language of emotion, developing detailed lexicons of feeling terms, and organized "families" of emotion words. Still others conducted laboratory research in which strong moods were induced in unsuspecting college students through film and music, and their impact on attention, memory, and problem-solving was measured. Some investigators focused on the self-regulation of emotion, and how to engage in it adaptively. In another far off corner of the research landscape, still other experimenters concerned themselves with how emotional processes go awry in mental disorders such as schizophrenia and depression. We published our 1990 article, called *Emotional Intelligence,* as a modest attempt to organize these various lines of research around a common framework. And, to communicate a message: Emotions and intelligence not only could co-exist, but they were interdependent. One couldn't be fully intelligent without appreciating, understanding, and working with emotion.

In 1990, not many people cared. But someone who did was Daniel Goleman, a *New York Times* journalist who was trained as a psychologist. In his 1995 bestseller, Goleman argued that an emotional intelligence was not just a novel idea, but one with important societal consequences. In his book, he called attention to the importance of learning about emotions in school, arguing that the prevention of student drop-outs, teenage pregnancy, and substance use, among other ills, might be enhanced if children were smarter about their emotions. Goleman highlighted two school-based programs: one called "Self-Science," an elementary school curriculum developed by a group of private school teachers in California who subsequently created an organization called Six Seconds; and the "Social Development Program," a multifaceted K through 12 curriculum featured in the New Haven, Connecticut public schools. These are interesting and remarkable examples of what has come to be known as SEL, Social and Emotional Learning programs.

Now, with the publication of their field-tested program, Maurer, Brackett, and Plain, have provided teachers and their students with an option, one that is more specifically developed for middle school level students and which focuses on the integration of emotion language and visual imagery as a way to motivate students to learn to talk about feelings – their feelings and those of other people – in their social environments. This 6-Step program to teaching emotional literacy is creative, engaging, and fun - it allows sophisticated and naïve students alike to build on their emotional skills and take them some steps further. I especially like the fact that the *Emotional Literacy* model can be infused into other subjects in the larger curriculum. What message do we convey to students when the only time we deal with emotions is at

11:00 a.m. on Tuesdays? Rather, this model, by enabling emotions to be seen in all domains of study, helps address the false dichotomy between mind and body, reason and passion, thinking and feeling.

Emotional Literacy in the Middle School reflects the coming together of emotion researchers and gifted educators to create a program that is understandable and easily implemented. It does not require anyone to learn an entirely new vocabulary or to engage in classroom exercises that some might find embarrassing or silly. Quite the contrary — if students and teachers are willing to consider simple pictures, tell stories, and reflect, they can enhance their emotional literacy.

The world our children have inherited is far more complex than the one in which we grew up. Many more distractions compete for their attention. Parents are busier than ever before, and schools are asked to play a role as social service centers that no one imagined even 30 years ago. Perhaps by enhancing skills concerned with understanding feelings, empathizing with the feelings of others, talking about them, and managing them in appropriate ways, our children will be helped to lead the kind of pro-social lives we could only have hoped for ourselves. I'm not going to claim that *Emotional Literacy in the Middle School* is the key to world peace, but perhaps it's a good place to start.

Peter Salovey, Ph.D.
Chris Argyris Professor of Psychology and Dean of Yale College

Preface

This book is not about declaring "war" on the latest problem borne out of alarmist statistics. It is not about a high profile, short-term program that must compete for public attention or funding. *Emotional Literacy in the Middle School – a 6-Step Program to Promote Social, Emotional and Academic Learning* is a well-designed, field-tested program that enhances social, emotional, and academic learning. It capitalizes on the general mission of schools: educating the whole child.

As educators we have long understood the importance of programs that enhance social and emotional skills. Yet, there has been good reason to regard these programs with skepticism and frustration. We have waged one "prevention" initiative after another, fragmenting our efforts into a succession of disjointed fads. We have been reactive, turning to cumbersome programs that are expensive to purchase, require extensive training, and demand time out of the classroom. We have learned concepts and theory but little about "how to." Most programs do not possess simple, effective teaching techniques; nor do they have enduring benefits beyond the classroom.

Emotional Literacy was designed to adhere to the guidelines of the Collaborative for Academic, Social, and Emotional Learning (CASEL) (see Elias et al., 1997; Payton, Graczyk, Wardlaw, Bloodworth, Tompsett, & Weissberg, 2000; Zins, Elias, Greenberg, & Weissberg, 2000). It teaches students to label, compare, and evaluate their own and others' thoughts, feelings, and actions, and to discuss and write articulately about social, academic, and personal experiences. It is also easily integrated into existing school curricula; it is theoretically based and developmentally appropriate; it is designed to promote a caring, supportive, and challenging classroom and school climate; and it promotes school, family, and community partnerships. The activities can help children cope adaptively with modern-day stresses, a skill which can potentially decrease or eliminate destructive behaviors.

This program is also designed to be teacher-friendly. It encourages differentiation of instruction, provides individualized learning in a classroom setting, and addresses each student's unique thinking and learning style. There is also training and support for teachers, an important factor in implementing programs successfully (Gottfredson & Gottfredson, 2002). Each school that utilizes the program can be systematically monitored and evaluated.

Unlike some traditional classroom learning where all students arrive at the same or similar conclusions, *Emotional Literacy* uniquely individualizes each student's learning experience. Students develop the ability to relate through subjective and vicarious means to human circumstances that far exceed their own limited references. Moreover, after completing the program, students have much more than a basic understanding of feeling words. Among the many benefits, students can identify, compare and evaluate their own and others' thoughts, feelings, and actions, understand the main idea of stories, describe real-life events and problems, and discuss and write articulately about social, academic, and personal or emotional experiences. Feeling words have now become an important device to help students gain control and govern their lives in a purposeful and productive manner. A single word has become a world!

The lessons in *Emotional Literacy* go beyond traditional memory-based learning and logical-abstract thinking that are emphasized in today's schools. Results of the program are powerful, dramatic, and time-tested. This is demonstrated in the newspaper article abstracted below, which dates back to the early 1980's when the program was first pilot-tested (Schoenberg, 1981, p. 8):

> One sixth-grader walked into class with a cardboard doll representing the man accused of shooting President Reagan. Opening the chest, she revealed its paper heart, bearing the quote: "I suppressed so much that I had to explode." This student at an Upstate New York Middle School constructed the revealing doll as part of a program created by her teacher, Marvin Maurer, to help children better understand themselves and others.

> The topic for that week's "Little People Feeling Words" program was John W. Hinckely Jr., the 25-year old drifter accused of shooting President Reagan and three others. This was just one of many lessons for students to write and discuss their feelings pertaining to social issues and personal experiences. Encouraging students to more freely express their feelings is the major goal of the program. In essays and classroom discussions, the students suggested the tragic shooting might have been avoided if Hinckely had been better able to openly express his feelings.

> "He would be a person who suppresses and internalizes his emotions to a point that he had to explode by trying to assassinate the President," wrote Marnie.

> Sean's description of the incident was "I feel a lot of strong emotions but the one I feel the most is despair. I feel despair because I know that everybody doesn't agree with everybody else. Everybody has a different opinion and there's always a jerk who has to use a violent act to have his way out, and to me it seems like it will never stop."

> Melissa saw the problem as beginning with Hinckley's relationship with his family. "Children and parents should have intimate relationships," she wrote. "If his parents will not talk to him, the parents probably don't care enough to take him for medical help. After a while, it builds up so much anger that he

takes it out on someone he dislikes or he resents his mother and father."

Danny was sympathetic. "He might have had a rough childhood. Something might have made him enraged. He might have tried to suppress his feelings and emotions and he just couldn't hold them in anymore."

"I feel maybe he was insecure before he committed this crime and when he was younger, he suppressed his emotions from the world and he had to let it all out and shoot the president," wrote Sandy.

The students used these and other "feeling" words to describe Hinckely: alienated, hostile, insecure, enraged, identify, internalize, despair, angry, masochistic, and suppressed. Unlike the reactions of many adults, the children viewed the accused man sympathetically rather than angrily.

Twenty years later, this program was used to help children cope with the shocking events of September 11, which took a major psychological and emotional toll on the nation. The following article, entitled "Emotional Literacy and Alienation," appeared in the *New Jersey Star Ledger.* It described how a class of sixth grade students vocalized their thoughts and feelings concerning 9/11 and terrorism.

Students quickly turned the discussion from classroom bullies and school violence, to the United States' military offensive in Afghanistan. Alienation remained the focus of the discussion.

"People who live over there are being corrupted by their government, they're alienated from the truth," offered Kevin Fenstemaker, one of about 20 students in Courtney Roeser's class. "And Pakistan is alienating refugees from Afghanistan who want to escape bombings."

Added classmate Samantha Solomon, "There are many people in those countries that want to alienate themselves from their countries. I'm glad I'm not there but I feel real sorry for their people."

Following this discussion, students explained how they personally had felt alienated in certain situations. "I had a good friend who said nasty things about me. I felt really sad, angry, and alienated." The students seemed to understand the pain and anguish associated with different kinds of alienation.

The need for emotional literacy is unquestionable. As Daniel Goleman (1995, p. 263) wrote in *Emotional Intelligence*, "bringing emotional literacy into the classroom makes emotions and social life themselves topics, rather than treating the most compelling facets of a child's day as irrelevant intrusions or, when they lead to eruptions, relegating them to occasional disciplinary trips to the guidance counselor or the principal's office." *Emotional Literacy* is a program that educators cannot afford to dismiss or ignore.

INTRODUCTION and PROGRAM GOALS

You (the teacher) are central to this program's success. It is your enthusiasm that will bring emotional literacy to life with students in the classroom. Although some teachers feel overburdened by incorporating additional material into their classrooms, we are confident that you will recognize the positive changes that *Emotional Literacy* will bring to the students. Indeed, while some teachers are reluctant at the outset to tackle a topic such as emotional literacy that is foreign to their training, most feel positive after doing so. For example, one study in New Haven, CT, found that more than 90% of the teachers said they were pleased with an emotion-based, social development program and wanted to incorporate it again after the first year, even though 31% were reluctant initially (see Goleman, 1995).

Our program, *Emotional Literacy in the Middle School: A 6 Step Program to Promote Social, Emotional and Academic Learning,* is easily implemented because lessons are infused into subjects (e.g., language arts, social studies). This avoids overburdening teachers and students with more demands. Teachers and students have been consistently happy with the program. Students enjoy *Emotional Literacy* because the program addresses them as individuals, including their specific social, emotional, and academic needs. They also begin to feel more secure in expressing themselves without the fear of being judged and criticized. Teachers also see changes in themselves: they become more comfortable sharing their own experiences, better at responding constructively to their students' social and emotional needs, and are more keenly more aware of the special moments that help to maintain a healthy climate in the classroom. In addition, teachers notice in their students a decline in problem behavior and an increase in pro-social behavior in their classrooms.

In sum, many students have thoughts and feelings, which for various reasons remain unspoken or unexpressed. As professionals, we know some of these thoughts and feelings can lead to emotional distress and compromised learning. *Emotional Literacy* provides a format to help students express themselves intellectually and emotionally. This kind of interaction creates an atmosphere of togetherness in the classroom, which translates into positive learning. And positive learning can be correlated with increased achievement and improved proficiency related to academic standards.

Emotional Literacy is recommended for students in the middle grades, which can range from 5th-8th grade. Transfer students not present at the beginning of the school year will need only brief tutorial time. The curriculum can be used as a stand-alone program or it can be introduced to students as part of their general literacy studies in any content area; i.e. vocabulary, comprehension, oral and written expression, incorporating it as part of the normal lesson plan. Each lesson (after the first 3 lessons) follows a similar format.

The value of this program becomes clear and unquestionable when one reviews the intended student outcomes/program goals listed below. Through participation in this program, students will:

- Acquire a rich vocabulary to identify, label, and express diverse emotional experiences
- Develop self- and social- awareness
- Discern one's own emotional state and those of others
- Gather information on other's perspectives, enabling students to feel with and for others
- Understand the relationships between thoughts, feelings, and actions
- Learn what is "behind" feelings (e.g., the loneliness that can underlie alienation)
- Realize that people don't always show or express emotions and feelings accurately or similarly
- Perceive the changes and different intensities in moods and feelings
- Understand that one has the right to his or her own feelings
- Share and communicate thoughts and feelings with peers, parents, and teachers
- Choose appropriate emotional/behavioral responses in given situations
- Resolve personal conflicts and social difficulties in a productive manner, using words instead of destructive physical actions
- Build trusting relationships, become more empathic, and learn that others feel similarly in given situations
- Employ creative processes to enhance cognitive, social, and emotional development
- Write creatively and articulately about significant social, academic, and personal issues
- Improve critical thinking and decision-making skills
- Read materials with greater understanding, which helps performance on standardized tests
- Experience individualized learning in a traditional classroom setting: no student arrives at the same conclusion in any of the prescribed tasks

Program Overview

Learning in schools has been and still is primarily focused on what are popularly thought to be "left" hemispheric functions. For example, students typically learn vocabulary words by performing rote activities such as writing words and their definitions multiple times, using words in generic sentences, and employing mnemonic devices. In fact, in one school a teacher had 14-year-old students learning definitions of vocabulary words by mechanically reciting them over and over (Clott, 1998). Introducing words in the above manner does not facilitate the transfer of learning; it actually interferes with the subsequent development of understanding. Most likely the words will not be integrated into the student's repertoire but will be quickly forgotten.

Learning, storing, and remembering are dynamic-interactive processes. Language is not stored intact in one area of the brain. Instead, it is stored in pieces and distributed in sites throughout the brain. Therefore, the more connections that are made, the more understanding and meaning that can be attached to the learning experience. Regarding *Emotional Literacy*, recent research indicates that memories are coded to specific events and linked to both social and emotional situations (see Elias et al., 1997).

Emotional Literacy engages the intellectual, emotional, and social framework of the individual. Incorporating activities such as self-reflection, analysis of academic material and current events, classroom discussions, interaction with family members, artistic designs, and creative writing assignments – words become whole concepts – with many kinds of human implications. The **6 Steps** of this program create a complete and holistic understanding of words, which dramatically increases the probability of long-term storage and spontaneous usage.

Educators, particularly those who teach children from minority backgrounds, have long criticized the standard school curriculum. They question why children would be motivated to learn if they cannot relate what they are taught to their everyday experiences.

In **Step 1,** *Introducing Feeling Words* students are introduced to feeling words through specific questions that evoke anecdotal (personal) responses. For example, when introducing the word *alienation*, the following question is proposed to the class: "Has anyone ever been *left out* of something, like not being invited to a party or to participate on a sports team?" Introducing words using questions that evoke anecdotal responses helps students to make personal connections to course materials. Essentially, the learning experience is organized and presented in a way that relates to each student's existing knowledge base.

Step 2, *Designs* and *Personified Explanations* departs from traditional teaching methods that focus on the cognitive, analytical, and convergent functions thought to be dominated by the left side of the brain. In this step, students make the connection between *Designs* (symbolic representations of words) and *Personified Explanations* (sentences that explain relationships between *Designs* and words) for each feeling word. *Personified Explanations* assign human qualities to the configurations within the *Design*. See Figure 1 below for an example of the word alienation.

Figure 1: *Design* and *Personified Explanation* for the word: *Alienation.*

Personified Explanation: The circle is *alienated* from the triangle by the line.

Analyzing the configurations within a *Design* requires students to visualize the elements and actions that represent the words' meaning (i.e., the line separates the triangle from the circle = *alienation*). When students engage in this process, something quite fascinating happens: the word is being analyzed intellectually, emotionally, and spatially. Incorporating *Designs* and *Personified Explanations* fosters creative, intuitive and spontaneous expressions.

History, literature and current events invariably involve characters and individuals who become happy, sad, angry, fearful, hateful, and so forth. In **Step 3, *Real World Association - RWA*,** students research and write sentences using feeling words pertaining to significant social and academic issues (e.g., literature, history, current news story). Students then diagram the *RWA* using the original *Design*, as depicted in Figure 2. For example, when studying the Holocaust, students can evaluate different aspects of WWII from both an intellectual and an emotional perspective. This exercise teaches students to evaluate how people and groups on local, national and international levels express and manage their emotions, whether positive or negative.

Figure 2: *Real World Association* and *Design* for the word: *Alienation*

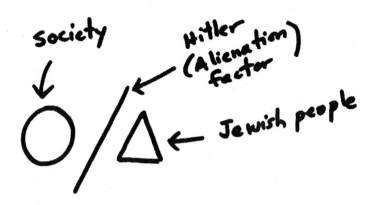

RWA: During W.W. II, the Jews in Europe were *alienated* from the German society because of Hitler's anti-Semitic beliefs.

Children need to learn to share thoughts and feelings, as part of maturing. Therefore, in *Step 4, Personal/Family Association- PFA,* students discuss feeling words and their relationships with personal experiences at home with family members. For example. when learning about the word *alienation,* a child could ask a parent if he or she ever felt *alienated,* and why, when? The family-child discussion leads to the writing of one or more *PFA(s).* Students may choose to write about their own personal experience or, with permission, about the personal experiences of a family member. When students relate feeling words to their own private experiences and those of others, they gain more insight into the significance of the human experience. Students also become more comfortable disclosing private feelings with family members and come in contact with a broader spectrum of human experiences to which they may not ordinarily be exposed. Learning becomes a family affair.

Developing satisfying relationships, enhancing decision-making skills, and dealing with peer pressure, all involve interaction and communication with other people. In **Step 5,** *Classroom Discussions*, students share their *RWAs* and *PFAs* with their teacher and classmates. When students share their work, they gain a sense of ownership in the classroom because they are making a significant contribution to the learning experience. In addition, by hearing multiple perspectives, students greatly increase their overall emotional knowledge-base and develop more honed personal views.

Students complete *Creative Writing Assignments* in **Step 6**. Although the teacher chooses both the topic and the specific feeling word(s), the direction of the essay is the student's responsibility. Conclusions that children arrive at on their own are more personally and educationally meaningful than those proposed by others. In addition, by incorporating their own ideas and personal experiences (versus copying information from a textbook) into essays, students gain more confidence in their writing ability, and more insight and clarity as to what they think and feel about themselves and others. Writing about personal experiences also promotes physical health and well-being.

Below is one sixth grade girl's short essay concerning the feelings of Julius Caesar - with one historical difference – Caesar knows Brutus is out to get him. The assigned words were *alienation* and *depression*. Notice how the student chose to add the following feeling words: *secure, despair, stunned,* and *trust.* Pay particular attention to how the student juxtaposed words like *pool* and *despair*, and how the word *alienation* is used metaphorically.

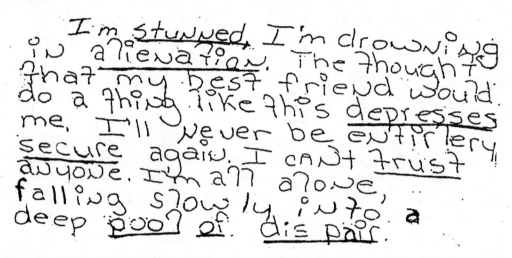

In addition to the **6 Steps**, there are larger ***Student Projects***, which are designed to have students work intensely on emotional literacy skills. The projects are tailored to specific social and emotional competencies, including the perception of emotion in others and the regulation of emotion in oneself and others. For example, there is a project in which students peruse newspapers and magazines for pictures pertaining to the expression of basic and complex emotions. They then create collages or mobiles to publicly display various emotions. In another project students identify a song and think about; (a) the lyrics of the song, (b) what the artist/band may have been thinking and feeling when writing the song, and (c) the feelings the song evokes (both the lyrics and music), among other things. Students then write a story about the emotional content of the song. They also have the option to share projects with the class.

GENERAL INSTRUCTIONS

In preparation for beginning the program, it is suggested that teachers:

1. Read this book through in its entirety; create variations/options to address the unique needs of the students.
2. Review the Program Overview & General Instructions carefully, as well as the At A Glance section.
3. Practice lessons 1-3 privately or with peers/colleagues/ family members to gain familiarity and ease of instruction.
4. Become familiar with the *Teacher Lesson Sheets/Student Worksheets*.
5. Mail parent letter (Appendix D) to students' homes prior to starting the program.
6. Start the program no earlier than the 5th or 6th week of school so as to give the students and teacher a chance to get to know one another.

It is also recommended that teachers inform students that they will be starting a program that will focus on people's emotions and feelings. The students should know that there will be lots of fun assignments and that a lot of their work will be used for class discussions, writing assignments, and other projects. Students should also be aware that there are some ground rules. Because some of the information that students will share is private, it is important for them to understand the importance of confidentiality in the classroom. Of course, they will be encouraged to share and discuss feelings and issues that arise, but this should never be at the expense of another student. Students should be aware that making fun of another student's feelings or perspective on a topic will not be tolerated and that they should "treat others as they would like to be treated themselves." In our experience, students rarely make fun of students who share personal experiences in the context of the program.

In the past, these rules have helped to establish an atmosphere of trust and togetherness in the classroom, which translates into a positive learning environment.

Key Points Before Starting the Program
1. The first 3 Sample Lessons of the program introduce one word per day. This will help students become familiar with the steps, particularly, **Step 2** (*Designs* and *Personified Explanations*). After the three lessons, all other lessons follows a similar format.
2. We recommend that 2 words be introduced each week. The program is designed to take approximately 30 weeks or one school year to complete.
3. For the duration of the program, two words should be introduced at a time on one day, early in the week (i.e., **Steps 1 & 2**). Teachers may introduce the words in order or choose the words randomly to fit into topics of study across

content areas. *Alternate forms of each word may and should be used.*

4. **Steps 3 and 4** are assigned for homework. The students may be given 1 - 2 days to complete the homework assignment, which leads to *Classroom Discussions* (**Step 5**) on the second day of instruction for the program that week.

5. On the 3rd instructional day, one or both words are incorporated into an essay. Students should be encouraged to use previously learned feeling words in essays in addition to the assigned words for that particular topic. The topic of the essay must be tailored to the feeling words of that week. It should allow for the incorporation of factual data as well as creative interpretation.

6. About 1 student project should be introduced every 4 weeks (after the first month).

Important Side Notes

1. The definitions being used relate only to the "emotional" meanings of the words. The authors' note that some words have many definitions.

2. Teachers should allow sufficient time for students to come up with responses (teacher pause).

3. Caution is urged in being *overly directive* with the program.

4. In the event a student becomes inappropriately personal, the teacher should sensitively conclude the dialogue and privately address the situation with the student/principal/parent.

AT A GLANCE SUMMARY

Instructional Day 1 (5-10 minutes): Introduce 2 feeling words **(Step 1)** and the *Designs* and *Personified Explanations* for both words **(Step 2)**; assign *Real World* and *Personal/Family* **(Steps 3 & 4)** for homework.

Instructional Day 2 (15 –20 minutes): *Real World Associations* and *Personal/ Family Associations* are done for homework; these are followed by *Classroom Discussion* **(Step 5)**.

Instructional Day 3 (20 – 30 minutes): Creative Writing Assignments are completed **(Step 6)**.

Monthly – Student Projects

Sporadically – "What's on your mind?" self-awareness activity

STEP	STRATEGY SEQUENCE	HELPFUL HIGHLIGHTS
-1- *Introduction of Feeling Words* Approximately 2-5 minutes per word PURPOSE: Connect feeling word to personal experience	a. Teacher poses question b. Teacher pause c. Sharing of anecdotes d. Introduction of word e. Word & definition in sentence form written on board by teacher f. Word and definition copied into student worksheets	Done on first instructional day Teacher interjection of anecdotes (determined by time factors and teacher discretion) The teacher should briefly continue discussion of a student response when it is apparent that the desire to elaborate is present. However, a question or comment is sufficient.
-2- *Designs* **and** *Personified Explanations (PE)* Time as needed PURPOSE: Symbolic representation of the feeling words	a. *Design* is drawn on the blackboard b. Students are asked to make a connection between the *Design* and the word c. Teacher writes *PE* on the blackboard d. Writing of students' own *PE's* in worksheets	Done on first instructional day The teacher should make sure that students see the connection between the *Design* and the *PE*
-3- *Real World Associations (RWA)* 10-20 minutes per word to complete assignment at home PURPOSE: Apply feeling words to social & academic issues *(RWA)*	a. Students write one or more sentences b. Students diagram *RWA* using original *Design*	Done as classroom activity through Lesson 3 and then assigned for homework beginning with *word* 1 No personal pronouns Demonstration of "how or why" 3 options: relation to school subject, social issue, or own frame of reference Basis for *Classroom Discussion* in **Step 5**

STEP	STRATEGY SEQUENCE	HELPFUL HIGHLIGHTS
-4- ***Personal/Family Assoc.(PFA)*** Discussion per word: 10-20 minutes at home. PURPOSE: Connecting personal and family experiences to feelings words	a. At home, students show & discuss *RWA* with family members b. Discussion moves toward personal c. Discussion focuses on personal experiences relating to new word d. Student writes a *PFA* pertaining to self or family member	Done as classroom activity "family groups" through Lesson 3 and then assigned for homework beginning with word 1 +Send home parent/ guardian/family letter Must address "private life" Demonstration of how, when, why, because Optional for student to share *PFA* with class
-5- ***Classroom Discussions*** Time frame determined by level of enthusiasm and teacher discretion. PURPOSE: *Classroom Discussions: RWA & PFA*	a. Sharing of *RWA*s and *PFA*s by students b. Selection of topic(s) by teacher based on above for discussion c. Question prompts from teacher d. *RWA* & *PFA* are "checked" as teacher calls upon students	Done on second instructional day (after students complete *RWA* and *PFA* for homework) Students may be placed into small groups at first to facilitate comfort in sharing Teachers should use student *RWA* and *PFA* as the jumping off point for discussion
-6- **Creative Writing Assignment** Approximate time: 10-15 minutes. PURPOSE: Judge how well the words have been assimilated into the students' repertoire	a. Assigned in class at discretion b. Teacher chooses social issue, course content, or *RWA* or *PFA* c. Assign one or more feeling words related to topic of essay d. Essays should be approximately half a page e. Critiques should always be positive f. Judge on connection to assigned task g. Use non-traditional symbols: O for OK, G for good, T for terrific h. List common errors & review with entire class	Assigned at discretion of teacher on second or third day Focus is on content & validation of student Emphasis is on creativity not "grammar" Students may add other words Essays may be introduced in any content area associated to the feeling words Teachers should spend about 1 minute scanning each essay
Student Projects	a. Assigned as a weekend project or class project b. Projects are done independently or in small groups c. Grading procedures are at the teacher's discretion	Assigned one per 4 to 5 weeks after first month of program Emphasis is on creativity and students' ability to adhere to the rules of the assignment.

The Essence of Emotional Literacy

- **What is Emotional Literacy?**

- **The Need for Emotional Literacy:**
  Preparing children for future challenges

- **What are Feeling Words?**

What is Emotional Literacy?

The most profound and important experiences in our students' lives are saturated with emotion. To name a few, children experience joy after accomplishing a difficult task, grief at the loss of a loved one, anger when treated improperly, and anxiety before taking a test. Children also experience mixed or multiple emotions about events in their lives: a child who is promoted into an honors English class may simultaneously feel pride, excitement, and nervousness; whereas another child who is an underachiever may feel anger, sadness, and rejection (among a multitude of other emotions). Positive emotions (e.g., joy, enthusiasm) usually arise when children progress toward a goal, whereas negative emotions (e.g., anger, despair) usually arise when children have difficulty accomplishing a goal. In essence, emotions are a wakeup call; they tell us to tend to something important in ourselves or our environment.

Emotions lie at the core of mental health. The most common complaints that lead children to therapy are depression and anxiety (Davidson & Cacioppo, 1992). Therefore, the capacity to understand emotions and deal with them effectively is an essential element of good health. Emotions are not our enemies; they are our allies, they need attention. Every day we experience dozens, and sometimes hundreds, of variations of emotions. These emotions are identified and distinguished by their unique feeling and accompanying thoughts, psychological and biological states, and associated behaviors.

Collectively, we have hundreds of words in the English language to express our emotions; nonetheless many children have difficulty describing their emotional experiences to others (Saarni, 1999). Children need to have the appropriate language for in-depth conversations and self-expression. Inability to communicate disconnects children from their peers and the adults around them.

Historically, emotions were seen as processes that disrupted rational thought and decision-making. For example, the Stoic philosophers of ancient Greece argued that emotions were unreliable and idiosyncratic sources of information (Lloyd, 1978). But now educators and psychologists are aware that emotional illiteracy can be maladaptive and cause problems in life. Neuroscientists, for instance, have shown that people who can no longer process emotional information due to brain injury have difficulty making decisions and managing their lives (e.g., Damásio, 1994). Moreover, research shows that some people handle their emotions better than others, which has important consequences (Brackett & Mayer, 2003). For example, individuals who are otherwise very intelligent sometimes make disastrous decisions because they fail to take into account their own and others' feelings. Bright politicians, for instance, can lose elections because their emotional reactions come across as inappropriate (Lopes & Salovey, 2004).

This publication, *Emotional Literacy in the Middle School,* is grounded in new theories of intelligence, which champion the idea of broadening what it means to be "smart" to include people's emotional and social competencies. This includes emotional intelligence (Mayer & Salovey, 1997; Salovey & Mayer, 1990) and intra-and interpersonal intelligences (Gardner, 1983/1993). Emotional intelligence pertains to the ability to perceive emotions, use emotions to facilitate thinking, understand emotions, and regulate emotions to enhance personal growth. Research on emotional intelligence shows that it: (a) represents a coherent and interrelated set of mental abilities that are distinct from traditional IQ measures, (b) predicts important behaviors including positive relationships and less drug and alcohol use, and (c) develops with age and experience (Brackett & Mayer, 2003; Mayer, Caruso, & Salovey, 1999).

Studies on emotional intelligence have shown that this ability relates to important social outcomes. Among school children, emotional intelligence has been associated with lower peer ratings of aggressiveness, higher teacher ratings of pro-social behavior, and less tobacco and alcohol consumption (Rubin, 1999; Trinidad & Johnson, 2002; Trinidad, Unger, Chou, & Johnson, in press). Among adolescents, emotional intelligence is positively related to higher self-reported empathy and well-being, and higher-quality relationships rated by peers and parents. Lower emotional intelligence, on the other hand, is associated with drug and alcohol consumption, social deviance and poor relationships (Brackett & Mayer, 2003; Brackett, Mayer, & Warner, 2004; Ciarrochi, Chan, & Caputi, 2000; Lopes, Brackett, Nezlek, Schütz, Sellin, & Salovey, in press).

There is now abundant evidence that the abilities to read emotions in faces, understand emotional vocabulary, and regulate emotions are associated with social competence and adaptation, as rated by peers, parents, and teachers (for reviews see Eisenberg, Fabes, Guthrie, & Reiser, 2000; Feldman, Philippot, & Custrini, 1991; Halberstadt, Denham, & Dunsmore, 2001; Saarni, 1999). Children who are viewed as emotionally literate by teachers and parents are also likely to behave in socially appropriate, non-aggressive ways at school and are likely to be relatively popular, pro-social and socially secure (Nellum-Williams, 1998). And evaluations of intervention programs emphasizing emotional competencies indicate that training emotional skills contributes to social adaptation and children's positive identification with their school (Elias et al., 1997; Hawkins, Catalano, Kosterman, Abbott, & Hill, 1999).

Emotional abilities are also important for academic achievement (Salovey & Sluyter, 1997; Weissberg & Greenberg, 1998). One major goal of the educational community is to help students become critical thinkers who are able to analyze, synthesize and evaluate information. Critical thinking, however, cannot be separated from emotional abilities. Perceiving and understanding emotions may be important for interpreting literature and works of art. Using emotions may help students decide what activities to focus on. For instance, it may be easier to write a creative essay if one is in a good mood, because positive moods enhance divergent thinking and imagination. Negative or neutral moods on the other hand, may facilitate careful attention to detail and be suitable for more detailed work (Palfai & Salovey, 1993). Understanding emotions helps children develop a good command of language, communicate effectively, and analyze the characters and plot of a novel. Finally, the ability to manage emotions may help students handle anxiety-arousing situations, such as taking tests (Lopes & Salovey, 2004).

Emotional Literacy provides lessons which teach children how to: (a) recognize their own and others' emotions, (b) use their emotions to enhance thinking, (c) understand the language of emotions, (d) appropriately label emotions with words, (e) accurately express emotions, and (f) regulate or manage their own and others' emotions.

Students acquire a "feelings" vocabulary through a series of classroom and homework assignments presented in 6 easy-to-follow steps. The activities include self-reflection, analysis of academic material and current events, family interaction, symbolic representations of words, classroom discussions, creative writing assignments, and independent and group projects. Academically, the program enhances students' vocabulary, comprehension, writing, creativity, and critical thinking. Socially, it develops students' self-awareness, empathy, communication competency, healthy relationships, and better decision-making. Together these abilities help students to improve academic performance, promote personal growth, and enhance the quality of interpersonal relationships.

Emotional Literacy brings each student's emotional and social life into the classroom, treating some of the most powerful aspects of the student's day as relevant and important (Goleman, 1995). It is designed to be infused easily into most subject areas. Unlike other programs that only focus on theory and research findings, this one presents teachers with six concrete "how to" steps for quick and easy implementation. The program is also a preventative tool to help inoculate children against rising perils, such as substance abuse, victimization, and dysfunctional relationships in school and at home. It equips children to make intelligent decisions and perceive reality, not through the influences of others, but through their own developed capacities. Ultimately, the program increases the probability of children having quality interpersonal relationships and improved academic performance.

The Need for Emotional Literacy in Middle School: Preparing Children for Future Challenges

Adolescents, between the ages of 10 and 15, experience many predictable stresses and dramatic life changes - all of which profoundly influence, and in some instances, disrupt their academic performance and psychosocial functioning. The onset of puberty brings rapid increases in height and weight, hormonal changes, and cognitive maturation. The family, which previously had the strongest influence, is largely replaced by peer groups, which become the most influential source affecting students' behavior and values. Additional stresses and challenges are introduced during the transition from elementary school to the less structured middle school. Adolescents must contend with increased academic responsibility, and crucial decisions pertaining to appropriate friendships and experimentation with drugs and sex. The negative consequences of poor decision-making can lead to serious health and emotional problems that negatively affect the quality of adolescents' lives (Dryfoos, 1997; Weissberg, Barton, & Shriver, 1996).

In spite of several decades of heightened public awareness, many children's emotional and social skills are in decline. Teenagers say they feel increasingly alone and alienated, unable to connect with their parents, teachers and sometimes even classmates (Kantrowitz & Wingert, 1999). The current generation of children is more vulnerable than ever to the debilitating effects of depression and the associated problems of poor school performance, loneliness, and even physical illness (Martin, 1998). No children, rich or poor, are exempt. These problems are universal, occurring in all ethnic, racial, and socioeconomic groups.

Today's adolescents are taking more risks with their health, their lives and their future than ever before (Danish, 1997; Takanishi, 1993; Greenberg,Weissberg, et al., 2003). Maladaptive behaviors such as dropping out of school, smoking, using drugs, drinking alcohol, having unprotected sex, getting involved with gangs, and committing violence, are occurring at higher rates in younger age groups. In fact, in some of our city schools the drop out rate is approaching 50%. Eighth graders' use of marijuana has doubled since 1995. Between 9 and 13 percent of children ages 9 to 17 have serious mental or emotional disturbances (Federal Register, 1997). These problems substantially interfere with, or limit, our youths' ability to function effectively in the family, school, and community.

Possibly the most alarming data come from a study on children's emotional well-being. Researchers found both parents' and teachers' assessments of children's emotional skills are steadily taking a turn for the worse (Achenback & Howell, 1994). Children between the ages of six and sixteen functioned more poorly in the following ways:
> *Withdrawal or social problems:* preferring to be alone; being secretive; sulking often; lacking energy; feeling unhappy; being overly dependent.

Anxious and depressed: being lonely; having many fears and worries; needing to be perfect; feeling unloved; feeling nervous or sad and depressed.

Attention or thinking problems: unable to pay attention or sit still; acting without thinking; being too nervous to concentrate; doing poorly on school work; unable to get mind off thoughts.

Delinquent or aggressive: hanging around kids who get in trouble; lying and cheating; arguing a lot; being mean to other people; demanding attention; destroying other people's things; disobeying at home and at school; being stubborn and moody; talking too much; teasing a lot; having a hot temper.

Children who are deprived of learning appropriate and healthy ways of dealing with their emotions, and are unable to focus on constructive goals, may get involved in high-risk behaviors with serious and sometimes life-threatening consequences. Many youth develop negative future expectations and become less concerned about the dangers of high-risk behaviors because they do not feel valued by society. Until they feel valued and are given the chance to contribute to society, their operative response to involvement with problem behavior may become, "Why not?" On the other hand, youth with positive expectations for their personal futures tend to be at lower risk for engaging in problem behavior because they view their participation in conventional society as having long-range rewards (Gullotta, 1990).

Research has shown that children with conduct problems tend to regulate emotions with aggressive strategies in which they vent their anger (Brenner & Salovey, 1997). These children may rely upon these strategies to a greater degree because they have less insight into their own and others' emotional experiences. Unfortunately, their communication problems often lead to peer-rejection and social isolation, putting them in jeopardy for increased emotional problems, poor academic performance and heightened risk for delinquency.

When negative social and emotional forces are present in a child's life and not properly addressed, it is predictable that the child will have poor concentration, a lack of attention, and negative peer interactions. In general, such a child will be a disturbing influence at home, in school, and in his or her own progress. In *Student Brains and Classroom Learning*, David Sylwester (1998) asserts that learning cannot take place in isolation from children's emotions because emotion drives attention, which drives learning, memory, motivation, and behavior. In fact, scientists have discovered that it is biologically impossible to learn anything if attention is focused elsewhere. For example, under high levels of stress, the indexing capabilities of the brain are limited and short-term memory and the ability to form new permanent memories is suppressed (Jacobs & Nadel, 1985).

Children's social and emotional skills are first developed at home with good parent-child interaction. Children learn the importance of respecting and managing their own and others' emotions from their primary caregivers. This succeeds to a greater or lesser degree in each home. How caregivers respond to their children's feelings has a huge impact on children's ability to understand feelings and read them correctly in others. Parents who dismiss feelings or punish displays of appropriate emotions are setting their children up for problems (Gottman, 2001).

Today's parents, however, are spending less quality time with their children. The last two decades have brought many changes to American families and communities, which may contribute to our youth's problems (Hamburg, 1992; Greenberg, Weissberg et al., 2003). Working hours are longer, divorce is more prevalent, and extended families that live close to children are less common. Many children go home to an empty house after school, eat dinner alone or while watching TV, and listen to the radio while driving in the car with their parents. Furthermore, many of today's parents have little oversight of their children's peer relations and tend to not ask for school reports, monitor class assignments, or attend school activities (Orlich, Harder, Callahan, & Gibson, 1998). A majority of children spend additional hours each day playing video games and surfing the internet – usually alone. This leaves little to no time for parent-child communication.

With the family no longer offering growing numbers of children a sure footing in life, the prevalence of high-risk behavior on the rise, and increasing violence in the nation's middle and high schools, there is now, more than ever, an urgent need for prevention. However, the current trend to increase security and create fortresses where tragedies can never happen is misguided and impossible. How, then, do we improve children's social and emotional skills?

Researchers and educators recognize the importance of school-based health-promotion and social and emotional competence programs for early adolescents (Elias et al., 1997). Since virtually every child goes to school and spends a large percentage of the day with teachers and peers, what happens in the classroom can profoundly influence academic achievement and psychosocial development.

In *Promoting Social and Emotional Learning*, Maurice Elias and his colleagues asked, "Is it possible to attain academic and personal success without addressing social and emotional skills?" Accumulating evidence supports the answer: No! The common element among schools reporting an increase in academic success, improved quality of interpersonal relationships between teachers and students, and a decrease in problem behaviors, is a systematic process for promoting children's social and emotional learning (Elias et al., 1997). Moreover, new studies suggest that emotions play a crucial role in one's ability to make smart decisions (Vogel, 1997) and that emotional knowledge may play a role in the regulation of emotion (Eisenberg, Fabes, Murphy, Maszk, Smith, & Karbon, 1995). For example, when a young boy can accurately understand and express his angry feelings (freely, clearly, and constructively), he is less likely to get frustrated and resort to any form of self or other-directed destructive behavior in school.

Noted psychiatrist David Hamburg asserts that there is something different about those students who have had emotional literacy classes: they find the new pressures of peer politics, the upping of academic demands, and the temptations to smoke and use drugs less troubling than their peers. They have mastered emotional abilities that, at least for the short term, inoculate them against the turmoil and pressures they are about to face (cited in Goleman, 1995). Why then do so few schools have on-going programs to promote social and emotional learning?

Native intelligence, low socioeconomic status, minority background, or family disorganization cannot be continuously held responsible for children's behavioral problems and poor academic performance. *Emotional Literacy* can make the decided difference. It brings a human element to the impersonal buildings and institutionalized delivery systems of many public schools. *Emotional Literacy* sends an important message to students that can deeply affect their academic interest and motivation. It provides them with a firm foundation for their successful cognitive, social, emotional and behavioral development. *Emotional Literacy* enables schools to make a genuine commitment to support the full development of adolescents.

What are "Feeling" Words?

How many times have we all wanted to say something but couldn't find the right words? This is particularly evident when we have the need to express our likes, dislikes, and more complex emotional experiences. If the right words are not accessible, there is a break down in communication and our feelings can remain confused, unexpressed, suppressed or displaced. In many instances, poor communication leads to misunderstanding, which can end up in physical conflict.

Children seemingly have a need to put into words almost everything they experience. Words help them voice their internal states, ask for information, and get attention and affection. It is natural for children to want to communicate what makes them happy, sad, or angry and for them to want someone to hear what they say, in the way they intended. Underlying the reason to communicate is the need to make a connection with significant others. If this connection is not achieved, children may become angry, lonely, alienated or physically sick.

Young children use basic words to define their feelings: happy, sad, and mad. But older children need a much wider range of words in order to identify and express their feelings. *Emotional Literacy* introduces "feeling" words that characterize the gamut of human expression. The term "feeling" words is used to distinguish feelings, which pertain to the private, mental experience of an emotion, from emotions, which are observable in facial expressions and other forms of nonverbal behavior (cf. Damasio, 1994).

The feeling words for the program (Appendix A) were carefully selected from lists of fundamental and complex emotions that have been compiled by emotion researchers over the last few decades. (Plutchik, 1984). Included on the list are "positive" terms such as *jubilance* and *exhilaration*. Other words such as *masochism* and *envy* address "negative" feelings and behaviors. These words were included to help children understand the aberrant behavior and violence that are a part of our society. Also included are behavioral terms such as *commitment* and *motivation*. These words are not emotions per se, but they elicit emotional reactions before, during, and after an action. For example, a young girl doesn't "feel" motivated to become an Olympic athlete; it is her anticipated positive feelings such as joy and pride that motivate her to practice gymnastics everyday in order to try out for the Olympics.

In order for individuals to identify with and subsequently discuss or write about human circumstances, whether historical or contemporary, there is a need to find the "connecting link." Feeling words bridge the gap between one human life and another. They provide students with a non-violent alternative to resolve disagreements before they escalate into full-blown combat situations. Connecting words to feelings may also change the way a child's brain develops, forming links between the emotional and thinking parts of the brain (Caine & Caine, 1994; Sylwester, 1995).

Thoughts and feelings require words. Words, integrated and understood as concepts, serve as an important manipulative device to help students control and govern their lives in a satisfying and compatible manner. Depriving children of properly learning feeling words would be like removing one of the colors of a rainbow, not only would that single color be lost, but also the entire rainbow would be compromised.

Emotional Literacy Program

Step 1: Introduction of Feeling Words
Connecting Feeling Words to Personal Anecdotes

Step 2: *Designs* and *Personified Explanation*
Symbolically Representing Feeling Words

Step 3: *Real World Associations (RWA)*
Connecting Feeling Words to Social and Academic Issues

Step 4: *Personal/Family Associations (PFA)*
Connecting Personal and Family Experiences to Feeling Words

Step 5: *Classroom Discussions*
Sharing of Real World Associations and/or Personal/Family Associations

Step 6: *Creative Writing Assignments*
Incorporating Feeling Words into Open-ended Essays

Step 1
Introduction of Feeling Words:
Connecting Feeling Words to Personal Anecdotes

The objective of **Step 1** is to help students make a connection between personal experiences and the meaning of the new feeling word. The use of alternate forms of each feeling word should be encouraged...ex: *elation, elated; alienated, alienation*. This is accomplished by having students respond to certain prepared questions before the word is introduced. The questions personalize the learning experience and evoke anecdotal responses. Words introduced within the ambiance of an anecdote automatically link the new word to the student's previous experiences.

All teachers know that questions play a critical role in teaching. Knowing how to frame questions stimulates student thinking and guides them through the learning processes in a skillful and meaningful manner. A majority of questions that teachers pose, however, require only literal recall of information. Seldom is new material related to previously learned emotional or personal information. The questions in this program are constructed to help students recall emotional events and identify with personal experiences (i.e., anecdotal responses). This helps them relate to the word both intellectually and emotionally. Below are three sample questions for the first three feeling words in the program: *alienation, elated, and commitment.*

> Example 1: *Alienation*
> "When was the last time any of you (or someone you know) was left-out of something you really wanted to participate in - like not being invited to a party or not making the sports team?"

> Example 2: *Elated*
> "What were some of the most exciting times you've had (with your family, friends, at school, etc.)?"

> Example 3: *Commitment*
> "What are some important pledges or promises that we make in our lives?"

There are two important components in the above questions. First, they make use of each word's definition in easily understood language. Second, they elicit the desired emotional response by having students recall personal experiences related to the idea and meaning of the word.

After the teacher introduces the initial question to the class, there is generally a pause to allow students to recall and reflect on past experiences. Then the teacher asks for volunteers to share their anecdotes with the class. Below is an example of one boy's compelling response to the initial question concerning the word *alienation*:

Recall the Initial Question:
"When was the last time any of you (or someone you know) was left-out of something you really wanted to participate in - like not being invited to a party, or not making the sports team?"

Boy's Response:
"When I tried out for the football team the coach told me I was just too small. It made me feel really angry and left-out."

In the above example, the boy made the connection between the idea of the word *alienation* and his own personal experience of being left out (note: the word *alienation* had not yet been introduced). The entire class also experienced the idea and meaning of the word by listening to their classmates' anecdotes, as well as by reflecting on their own personal experiences.

Remember, anecdotal responses must accurately and completely answer the initial question. For example, if the above student were to omit, "It made me feel really angry and left-out" his response would have been incomplete. In our experience, if a student doesn't complete his or her response, a simple comment such as, "How did that make you feel?" will suffice.

At times students may be reluctant to respond to questions or they will demonstrate reticence when questions are presented. If this occurs, we recommend that the teacher shares a personal anecdote or a story related to the idea of the word. For instance, when introducing the word *alienation*, a teacher might state, "When I was about your age, I was left out of..." or "I remember this young boy who was really sad because he was left out of the team he wanted to be on and never got picked to be..." In general, it is beneficial for the teacher to interject anecdotes as often as possible. The more personal experiences the teacher shares with the class, the more "human" the teacher is perceived to be, which makes the students feel more comfortable in sharing their own personal experiences. Furthermore, a feeling of togetherness is brought into the classroom.

It is important to note that students may not be able to identify personally with some feeling words. For those words, we formulate the question in the third person. For example, when introducing the word *sadism*, which most students have not experienced, the teacher would state:

"There are some people who enjoy being cruel to others. Can you imagine such a person? What kind of person would be like this?"

Framing the question in the above manner avoids the possibility of making a student uncomfortable since an opinion or a reaction to the question is all that is required.

When students respond anecdotally it is natural for teachers to respond. For example, if a student speaks of having been separated from whatever or whomever, the teacher would react sympathetically by saying, for example, "It must have felt really bad being left out..." A mini-conversation can also take place. Finally, it is a good policy to repeat part of the student's response (as noted above) during the question-anecdote sequence. It tells students that you really care about them and are listening to them.

Time factors and teachers' discretion determine the number of anecdotes that can be shared for each word. If it appears that a student desires to elaborate on an anecdote, the teacher should briefly continue the interaction.

After anecdotes or opinions/reactions have been shared, the teacher introduces the word:

> Word Introduction (in own way):
> "There is a (fancy) word that describes what we've been talking about. The word is *alienation*. The word *alienation* means to be or feel separated from something or someone."

The teacher then writes the word and its definition in sentence form on the blackboard and the students copy this information onto their master worksheet. It generally takes two to five minutes to introduce a new word, depending on how many anecdotes are shared. Alternate forms of each word can and should be part of the discussion. Questions for all 60 words in the program are in the Teacher Lesson Sheets at the back of the book. In addition, Appendix C contains instructions for using this methodology to introduce traditional vocabulary words.

The Importance of Introducing Words in this Manner

In **Step 1**, students are not just passively sitting at their desks or attempting the rote task of memorizing a word's definition. This step incorporates visual, auditory, and kinesthetic activities, as well as anecdotal references.

Significant learning best takes place with information that connects to previously established intellectual and emotional references. If a personal connection is not achieved, the learning experience is essentially isolated and forgotten. When a word is introduced with anecdotal references the students' curiosity and attention are sustained. Students also automatically relate the idea of the new word to their own or someone else's experiences. These personal connections actively engage students in the learning process, which tends to increase learning, retention, and spontaneous usage of the feeling words. Finally, **Step 1** introduces the idea of sharing experiences, which is a fundamental component to emotional literacy. Sharing experiences creates an ambience of trust and bonding in the classroom and puts students in the right frame of mind for learning.

Step 2
Designs and *Personified Explanations*: Symbolically Representing Feeling Words

The objective of **Step 2** is to help students attain a deeper understanding of the new feeling word that was introduced in **Step 1**. This is achieved by having them study the relationship between *Designs* (symbolic representations of feeling words) and *Personified Explanations* (sentences that explain the relationships between *Designs* and feeling words).

Designs

Designs are a combination of geometric figures such as a square, circle, triangle or any other kind of line or squiggle that symbolically represents the feeling word. Figure 1 illustrates a *Design* for the word *alienation.* All *Designs* are accompanied by a *Personified Explanation,* which details the dynamic relationship between the *Design* and the feeling word.

Figure 1: *Design* for *Alienation*

Personified Explanation: The circle is *alienated* from the triangle by the line.

These *Designs* never look like pictures of people, places, or things. Pictures (e.g., face, tree, boat) tend to be directional and elicit intellectual responses. The *Designs* in this program are neutral and far less directional. They are interpreted through the language of feelings, which activate different areas of the brain. For example, when looking at the provided *Design* for the word *alienation* many creative processes are needed to discover the relationship between the circle, slash, triangle, and the feeling word. Pictures, like the four boys interacting in Figure 2, elicit an automatic intellectual appraisal of the action. Connecting words to *Designs*, as opposed to pictures, facilitates creative, spontaneous and intuitive responses - a major goal of Emotional Literacy.

Figure 2: *Designs* versus Pictures

The circle is *alienated* from the triangle by the line.

The sad boy on the right is *alienated* from the other boys because...

Personified Explanations:

Personified Explanations assign human qualities to the geometric shapes within a *Design* and illustrate the interaction of the *Design* and its relationship to the word. *Personified Explanations* are always written using the geometric names (i.e., circle, square, squiggle, etc.) in the *Design*. As can be seen in Figure 3, the circle and triangle are separated by the line. The student, having learned that the word *alienation* pertains to feelings of separation, proceeds to discover a relationship between the *Design* and the word's meaning. Figure 3 provides three possible *Personified Explanations* for the word *alienation*. Observe the connection between the *Personified Explanation* and the *Design*.

Figure 3: *Design* and Three *Personified Explanations* for *Alienation*

Personified Explanations:

1. The circle and the triangle feel *alienated* because they are separated from each other by the line.

2. The circle is *alienated* from the triangle by the line.

3. The *Design* looks like the word *alienation* because the circle is separated from the triangle by the line.

Notice the *Personified Explanations* contain the word 'by' or 'because'. This helps students to see the action in the *Design*.

Instructions

After introducing the word to the class in **Step 1**, the teacher draws the provided *Design* on the blackboard. The teacher then states (in own way), "Now that you know the definition of the word *alienation, commitment,* etc., can anyone describe in his or her own words how the *Design* looks like the word *alienation,* etc.?" After a few students respond, the teacher writes the *Personified Explanation* on the blackboard while the students copy it in their worksheets below the provided *Design.* If there is any hesitation, the teacher immediately proceeds to write the *Personified Explanation* under the *Design* while explaining how the *Design* relates to the word.

Importance of *Designs* and *Personified Explanations* when Learning Feeling Words

Toddlers, with pencils and crayons make all kinds of "designs" believing they are writing a story, and in actuality, they are. It is this creativity, so often stifled at an early age, that *Emotional Literacy* seeks to restore.

Step 2 makes use of what neuroscientists have recently discovered about the learning process. When a student concentrates on the *Design* and *Personified Explanation* there is greater involvement between the hemispheres. Generally speaking, the right hemisphere is more involved in visual, nonverbal, spatial, divergent and intuitive thinking (i.e., *Designs*), and the left hemisphere is especially activated by verbal, logical, categorical, detailed oriented, convergent thinking and analysis (i.e., *Personified Explanations*). The most productive intellectual functioning occurs when there is joint activation by both sides of the brain.

As can be seen in Figure 4 below, there are literally infinite ways to construct *Designs*. There are no right or wrong or good or bad ways to design a word. In fact, one *Design* can represent many words and vice versa. In fact, as an extra activity teachers can ask students to construct their own *Designs* and *Personified Explanations*.

Figure 4: Two Different *Designs* and *Personified Explanations* for: *Alienation, Commitment,* and *Elated.*

The circle is *alienated* from the triangle by the line.

The lone circle has been *alienated* from the group of other circles.

The circles are *committed* to each other because they will stick together and always help each other out.

The *Design* looks like the word *commitment* because the line will go in any direction to achieve its goal.

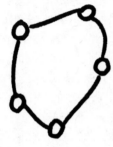

The circles are *elated* because they all won the game.

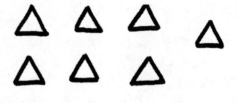

The triangle in front is *elated* because it has just been elected as the leader of the group.

Step 3
Real World Associations(RWA):
Connecting Feeling Words to Social and Academic Situations

The objective of **Step 3** (*Real World Associations - RWA*) is to have students make a connection between the assigned feeling word and the "real" world. Students write one or more sentences relating the feeling word to the real world everyday experiences of various characters or people with whom they come in contact. Academic subjects, including history and literature or important social events (local, national, or international level), or something the student feels strongly about, can act as references for the *RWA*. Using the original *Designs,* students then diagram their *RWA* by substituting the geometric configurations in the *Design* for the actual people, places and things in their *RWA*. Diagramming the *RWA* assures that students completely understand the feeling word and its association to the real world. We have provided three *RWAs* for the word *alienation* to show the different kinds of subject matter that can be employed (See Examples 1-3). Below is the original *Design* and *Personified Explanations* for the word *alienation* to show the connectivity of the steps.

Figure 1: Original *Design* for the word *Alienation.*

Personified Explanation: The circle is *alienated* from the triangle by the line.

Figure 2: *RWA* Example 1: School Subject Area – WWII

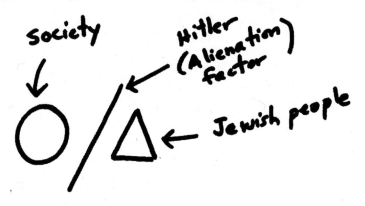

1a. During W.W. II, the Jews in Europe were *alienated* from the German society because of Hitler's anti-Semitic beliefs. (Complete)

1b. The Jews in Europe were *alienated* from the German society. (Incomplete)

Figure 3: *RWA* Example 2: Social Event - News Story

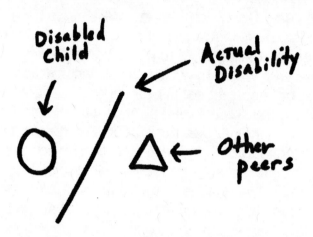

2a. Children with disabilities often feel *alienated* from their peers because they can't participate in regular physical activities. (Complete)

2b. Disabled children feel *alienated* from their friends. (Incomplete)

Figure 4: *RWA* Example 3: Social Event - International News

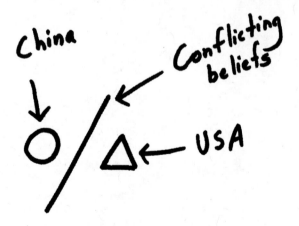

3a. China and the USA are *alienated* from each other because of different political and economic beliefs. (Complete)

3b. China is *alienated* from the USA. (Incomplete)

There are two important rules for the *RWA*. First, personal pronouns such as I, me, he, she, or we should not be used because they foster subjective responses which are reserved for **Step 4** *(Personal/Family Association)*. Second, the *RWA* and its diagrammatic component must demonstrate "how or why" the *RWA* relates to the *Design*. This was evident in the three incomplete *RWAs* above: the student's did not state "*by, because, how, why, etc.*" The reason these *RWAs* are incomplete is because there would be no assurance that students have a true understanding of the word.

Instructions

In the *RWA* homework assignment, students write one or more sentences relating the feeling word to (a) a school subject (i.e., history, literature, etc.), (b) a social issue on a local, national, or international level (i.e., they use magazines, newspaper articles, etc.), or (c) something of social importance to them (i.e., an event they witnessed). The teacher can either assign the topic (story, news article, etc.) for the *RWA* or give the students the freedom to choose between the three alternatives. The student always extrapolates the information to write the *RWA*. The goal is for students to arrive at their own conclusions, which are more meaningful than those proposed by others. For example, the *RWA* concerning Hitler's anti-Semitic beliefs was written by a student who had been studying World War II; the sentence about the disabled child was written by a student who was reading a newspaper story pertaining to the problems of the disabled; and the other child's explanation involving the political and economic conflicts between the USA and China was completed after reading a magazine article.

For the first three sample lessons, the *RWA* is done as a classroom activity to help students become acquainted with the process. Beginning with the fourth Feeling Word, the *RWA* is completed for homework. The homework is then used as the basis for Classroom Discussions (**Step 5**) and Creative Writing Assignments (**Step 6**). Students write the *RWA* directly on the *student worksheets* and then diagram the *design*.

The Importance of the *Real World Associations*

All history lessons, great literature and important social events invariably involve people who become happy, sad, angry, fearful, hateful, and so forth. When completing the *RWA*, students have the opportunity to evaluate people and groups and to observe what makes individuals feel as they do, as well as to learn how individuals cope in response to their feelings. The *RWA* also helps develop compassion and empathy, which are foundational to character development.

Relating feeling words to current events and significant social issues clearly reveals the need for people and nations to respect each other and helps students see the importance of interdependence. Additionally, it keeps children apprised of what is occurring in society and the changes to which global society is continuously subject. It is almost axiomatic that the more information students transfer from their schooling to everyday life, the greater the probability they will be good communicators, informed citizens, critical thinkers, and successful problem solvers.

Finally, the *RWA* is in keeping with the individualized learning concept that is an integral part of this program.

Step 4
The *Personal/Family Associations* (*PFA*): Connecting Personal and Family Experiences to Feeling Words

The objective of **Step 4**, the *Personal/Family Associations (PFA)* is to have students make the connection between the new feeling word and personal experiences. In this part of the program, students write about their own and/or a family member's (parent, caretaker, sibling) personal experience. After completing the *RWA* for homework, students are instructed to show and subsequently discuss the *RWA* with as many family members as possible. The discussion then graduates into a personal discussion between family members using the assigned word. The teacher should stress the importance of asking family members specific questions. The letter to the student's family should be sent out in advance (Appendix D).

Below is a sample scenario between a boy and his parents concerning the word *alienation*.

> "Mom/Dad, I just learned the word *alienation*. It means to be or feel separated from someone or something. I wrote about children with disabilities who often feel *alienated* from their peers because they can't participate in regular physical activities. What do you think about this kind of problem?"

A discussion then continues between the child and parents or caretakers; such discussion should include as many family members as possible. After the discussion the student tells the family member that the next step in the assignment is to discuss personal experiences pertaining to the new feeling word. For example, a student might state,

> "Mom/Dad, have you ever been *alienated* from something or someone?"

The child and parent/family member proceed to talk about personal experiences related to the new feeling word (i.e., share experiences related to the word *alienation*). After the family discussion the student writes one or more *PFAs* - pertaining to him/ herself or the student's family member.

Unlike the *RWA*, the *PFA* is "personal" and affords students the choice as to whether or not they will eventually share it with the class during the discussion period (Step 5). Below are three student's *PFAs* for the word *alienation*. The first is autobiographical and the second and third pertain to family members.

1a. When I was not allowed to participate on the football team, I felt *alienated* from the group, which made me feel somewhat depressed. (Complete)

1b. I felt *alienated* from the group. (Incomplete)

2a. My father felt very sad when as a teenager he was *alienated* from his friends because he failed the try-outs for the school band. (Complete)

2b. My father felt *alienated* when he was a teenager. (Incomplete)

3a. My sister Mary was *alienated* from her friends when she was not invited to go to the movies with them. She felt really angry with her sisters. (Complete)

3b. My sister Mary was *alienated* from her friends. (Incomplete)

There are two important rules for the *PFA*. First, it must address the "private life" of the student or the student's family member. Second, *PFAs* are only complete when students explain how, when, why or because in the sentence. As can be seen above, the child felt sad when he was *alienated* because he was not allowed to participate on the football team. In 1b. above, the *PFA* was incomplete because there was no assurance that the student understood the meaning of the word. And most importantly, he would have failed to express more of his feelings.

Instructions

For the first three sample lessons, the *PFA* is done as a classroom activity to help students become acquainted with the process. After the word is introduced and discussed, students can be put in small "family" groups. Students take turns practicing with their school family before going home to their real family. The teacher may assist students with their dialogue by role-playing. Another option is for the teacher to select a sample family group to model the process for the rest of the class. Beginning with the fourth feeling word, the *PFA* is completed for homework. Students record their responses directly onto the *Student Worksheet.* The homework is then used as the basis for *Classroom Discussions* **(Step 5)** and essays.

The Importance of the *Personal/Family Association*

People learn about other people as a result of learning about themselves. When students relate "feeling" words to their own private experiences or the personal experiences of others it helps them attain a major goal of this program: to get in touch with "who they are," and what they really think and feel. This in turn helps them make more informed decisions, which is a key skill in determining the quality of one's life.

When students document anecdotes about themselves or others for the feeling words in this program, they come in personal contact with a large spectrum of human emotions to which they would ordinarily not be exposed. They also gain more insight and dimension into the significance of their own feelings.

Learning as a Family Affair

Children's expectations of their abilities begin at home. Unfortunately, parents work long hours, leaving little time and energy to oversee their children's schooling and socialization. Most teachers, however, know the path to an enriching and successful learning experience - get parents involved! Active parents follow the development of their children, reinforce the expectations of the schools, and monitor child behavior and participation. In fact, parents' involvement in education is an integral part of the *No Child Left Behind Act of 2001* which advocates that every school encourage parental involvement and participation to promote social, emotional, and academic growth of children.

Below is a list of benefits students and their families can anticipate when working together.

- It affords parents, relatives, even friends, an insight as to what Emotional Literacy is and its importance in everyone's life.

- Parents become more familiar with what their children are learning and how they are functioning emotionally.

- Discussions of personal feelings and experiences can insure some of life's greatest gifts: bonding, trusting, and healthy attitudes.

- It creates an atmosphere and respect for interdependence. Everyone is involved in the learning process - there are no secrets.

- Family members and students assume the role of both student and teacher, which is an ideal environment.

- Family members can continue to achieve higher levels of intellectual, emotional and social skills.

- The student gains a sense of ownership and being in control of the learning experience.

- Family members learn more about each other, which promotes family compatibility as well as personal growth.

- Families that interact successfully prepare children to integrate successfully and compatibly into mainstream society.

Step 5
Classroom Discussions:
Sharing of the *Real World Associations* and/or *Personal/Family Associations*

The objective of **Step 5** is to promote social interaction and open discussions in the classroom. This is accomplished by having students share either their *RWA* and/or *PFA* with their teacher and peers. *Classroom Discussions* are a natural extension of the *RWA* and *PFA*.

Important Note on the *PFA* and *Classroom Discussions*

In the beginning some students may be hesitant to openly discuss their *PFA*. The *PFA*, however, is "personal" and affords students the choice as to whether or not they share it with the class. Some children have learned, at times painfully, that it does not pay to participate in class because other students may put them down by making sarcastic/hostile comments or even laughing at them. We recommend a teacher-initiated discussion precede the first open *Classroom Discussion,* setting the rules for discussion (i.e., no snide remarks or put-downs, etc.).

In our experience, students who are reluctant to share in class become more comfortable after hearing other students discuss their *RWA* and/or *PFA*. However, by just being good listeners students are learning and benefiting from the discussions since they have the opportunity to relate to their peers' experiences and reflect on their own experiences.

Instructions

On the second instructional day of the program, after students have completed the *RWA* and *PFA* for homework, the teacher organizes an open *Classroom Discussion* during which students share their homework assignments with the class. Homework can be checked by walking around the room and spot-checking students' papers or it can be collected. It is important that the teacher develops a system to make sure that all students get a chance to share their responses. After a few *RWAs* and/or *PFAs* have been shared, the teacher chooses one or a few students' examples to act as the foundation for the *Classroom Discussion* (i.e., the students *RWAs* and *PFAs* act as a jumping off point). Essentially, the teacher should pull key points and phrases from the students' responses. The teacher may also choose the *RWA* that is most appropriate for the social climate in the class (e.g., a fight that broke out the other day or a recent political event). Another way to come up with questions on the spot for a discussion is to identify with the student's *RWA* or *PFA* (i.e., the teacher applies the *PFA* or *RWA* to his/her own experiences).

If the assigned feeling word relates to a significant social issue the teacher may choose to prepare a few questions in advance for the discussion. Below are a few ways we have discussed the words: *alienated, elated, and commitment.* Each example contains sample questions for the classroom discussion (these are repeated in the first three lessons). Notice how this type of questioning elicits thoughts, feelings, personal experiences, and opinions of the student body. Whenever possible, questions should be asked to help resolve difficult issues.

Example 1a: *Classroom Discussion (RWA - Alienation)*
Student - Real World Association
"Children with disabilities often feel *alienated* from their peers because they can't participate in regular physical activities."

Teacher - Sample questions to initiate Classroom Discussion:
"How do you feel about disabled students being *alienated* from social activities? What can we all do to help someone with a disability become more actively involved with different activities? Has anyone here ever had a friend who was disabled? Can you tell us how you felt? What can we as individuals do to help make this student feel better about him/herself. How can we show our concern for his/her feelings?"

Example 1b: *Classroom Discussion (PFA – Alienation)*
Student - Personal Association:
"I felt *alienated* from my friends when my parents grounded me for coming home too late. They wouldn't let me go to the movies on Friday night."

Teacher - Sample questions to initiate Classroom Discussion:
"How many of you in the class have been grounded before? Why do you think you were grounded? Do you think it was fair to be grounded for coming home late? Why did you come home late? Does anyone have a suggestion as to how to please yourself and your parents?"

Example 2: *Classroom Discussion (RWA – Elated)*
Student - Real World Association:
"Julius Caesar was *elated* when he became a member of the Roman Oligarchy because he was able to help the poor Romans live a better lifestyle."

Teacher - Sample questions to initiate Classroom Discussion:
"Why is it important to help people whenever we can? Why do you think Julius Caesar was *elated* after helping the poor Romans? When people who are in need of help, receive it, how do you think

they feel? Has anyone here ever helped someone who really needed help? Can you tell us how it made you feel?"

Example 3: *Classroom Discussion (RWA – Commitment)*
Student - Real World Association:
"In the Lion King, Simba was *committed* to returning to his village because he wanted to insure the future of the Pride (the other lions)."

Teacher - Sample questions to initiate Classroom Discussion:
"Why do you think Simba was so *committed* to helping the Pride? How do you think the members of the Pride felt about Simba? Has anyone here ever been *committed* to anything? Can you tell us about it? Why do some people *commit* themselves to achieving their goals or helping others and other people make very few or no *commitments*? "

Suggestions for Setting up *Classroom Discussion*

1. If time and logistics permit, ask students to form a circle.

2. Arrange discussions so students are exposed to multiple perspectives by utilizing various student's *RWAs* and/or *PFAs*.

3. Students should be prepared to provide the necessary background information from their *RWA* by reading or discussing part of the book, magazine article, or news story, etc. used to complete the assignment.

4. After asking a question, call on one or a few students and then assume a passive role in the ensuing discussion. Such a technique teaches students to conduct classroom discussions more independently.

5. It is crucial that you not use subtle put-down tactics, regardless of how outlandish a student's point of view may seem or how different it is from what you expected.

6. When you call on a student, show courtesy to that student by listening attentively to him or her. Generally, this will influence the students to grant the teacher the same kind of respect. Allow sufficient time for initial responses and then probe for further information if necessary. By encouraging students to listen to one another, you encourage them to participate in a dynamic fashion. You also encourage peer reinforcement of positive, constructive classroom behavior.

7. Encourage non-volunteers. Try to determine why each non-volunteer remains quiet (i.e., is the student shy or does he/she have a language disability).

Many non-volunteers have learned, sometimes painfully, that it does not pay to say anything in class because the teacher or other students will put them down. No student will volunteer if a response may be met with sarcasm, snide remarks, or hostility.

8. Guard against the temptation to call primarily on bright, articulate, and assertive students. Try to include all students.

9. Occasionally a student will share a private experience and become ridiculed by his or her fellow students. For example, in one class, a boy disclosed that his worst fear was that he would grow up without any friends. After his comment to the class, a few students made derogatory remarks. In the event that this occurs, the teacher should turn the discussion around by asking students for suggestions to help with this problem.

Importance of *Classroom Discussions*

The importance of social interaction in the classroom cannot be overstated, not only between teacher and student but also among students themselves. Numerous studies have shown that when tasks are structured to encourage cooperation and interaction in the classroom, students greatly expand each other's knowledge base. In addition, students in discussion-based classes learn concepts and vocabulary better than students who only read instructional materials.

Classroom Discussions encourage students to share their thoughts, feelings, experiences, and opinions. The discussions improve listening skills and are instrumental in helping students better understand themselves and their classmates. Academic subjects become more exciting when discussed on a personal level and the nature of the content heightens students' interest and attention, which is crucial in learning and developing interpersonal relations. A sense of trust and bonding with others is also formed, which helps students feel part of a classroom family (as opposed to the feeling of isolation that many children encounter in school). There are added benefits for students who have not been exposed to people of different backgrounds - economic, ethnic, religious, and racial - and to ideas and perspectives that may be different from their own. Awareness of multiple-perspectives also helps students develop more honed personal views.

Learning to share one's thoughts and feelings has profound psychological benefits and is one of the key ingredients in developing satisfying relationships at home, in school and at the workplace. *Classroom Discussions* tend to lessen feelings of alienation by revealing that people's differences are far less important than their commonalities.

Classroom Discussions may also precipitate positive behavioral changes. For example, in one class, students discussed the transition to middle school and the difficulties they were anticipating upon arrival to the new environment. One sixth-grade girl rather shyly stated, "I'm afraid that I won't have a lot of the same friends in my class." Other students then shared their own feelings, many with similar sentiments. Prior to sharing their feelings, quite a few students felt the same anxiety as the girl. Afterwards, students felt more comfortable knowing that others had similar feelings.

Step 6
Creative Writing Assignments:
Incorporating Feeling Words into Open-ended Essays

A student's ability to write creatively with feeling words is one of the best ways to judge how well the feelings vocabulary has been assimilated into his/her repertoire. Writing short essays is also an invaluable tool to help students get in touch with and clarify their inner thoughts and feelings. In fact, many researchers assert that writing actively shapes children's thoughts and promotes social-cognitive and social-emotional development (e.g., Daiute & Buteau, 2002).

Instructions

The topic for the creative writing assignment is flexible. We suggest the teacher choose a topic from an important current or past social issue, a related school subject, or from students' *RWAs* or *PFAs*. Alternatively, a word-pair can be chosen (Appendix B) for the essay. If the word-pair option is chosen, the students are asked to write a story about themselves or someone else that clearly has a beginning, middle, and end.

There are undoubtedly hundreds of social issues that can be incorporated into the creative writing assignment (e.g., voting issues, political views, gangs, teen pregnancies, drug issues). As stated earlier, we have found that the common element between students and characters in history, literature, or contemporary society is their feelings. When students identify with people through the language of feelings they are more likely to become intimately involved with the writing assignment. Writing in this capacity links course content to the private lives of the students adding insight to their awareness of self and others.

Generally, students are assigned a short essay after two words have been introduced. Each essay must incorporate the feeling words related to the chosen topic. Students are always encouraged to add other feeling words that they have learned previously. Although the teacher chooses both the topic and the feeling words, the direction of the essay is entirely the student's responsibility, making each essay a unique creation.

The importance of the open-ended essays can be seen in those that follow. They were chosen from average 6th grade students in a rural community. All essays were written in about 15 minutes in class. None of these essays were edited. They are actual photocopies of each student's work.

Sample 1: History and Feeling Words

As described in the Program Overview, one teacher decided to have her class write a short essay concerning the feelings of Julius Caesar with one historical difference – Caesar knows Brutus is out to get him. The students were asked to identify with Julius Caesar's circumstances. The assigned words were: *alienation* and *depression*. Notice how the student added other feelings words: *'secure', 'despair', 'stunned',* and *'trust'*. Pay particular attention to how the student juxtaposed words like 'pool' and *'despair'* and how the word *alienation* is used metaphorically.

> I'm stunned, I'm drowning in alienation. The thought that my best friend would do a thing like this depresses me. I'll never be entirely secure again. I can't trust anyone. I'm all alone, falling slowly into a deep pool of dispair.

Sample 2: Important Social Issue

The teacher in this classroom asked students to write about the drug problems among students. In this instance the teacher assigned feeling words: *masochistic* and *frustration*. Notice how the student chose to add the idea of the person internalizing vs. externalizing his feelings as well as other feeling words.

> People who take drugs are really masochistic. They feel hostile towards people because they are frustrated and insecure. They internalize their feelings instead of externalizing them. They feel they are. in dispair or inferior to others. Once they take drugs they get hooked on them and are anxious to get on to real heavy dope like grass. They do not feel inappropriate about what they are doing. They think its right. They think, "Well maybe it will help, who knows?" And maybe — "Who cares?"

Sample 3: History and Current Events Combined

This next essay exemplifies how the past and present can be brought together through an appropriate question. Students were told: "You are a homoerectus man who has been frozen in a mountainside for the past 500,000 years. In some fantastic way, you are released and find yourself on the outskirts of New York City. As you begin to enter the city, you feel..." Notice how this girl is not limited by historic data and is free to express herself in a creative manner using the provided information and the feeling words:

Anxiety - Depression

As I entered the city a wave of negative expectations swept over me. Every thing here was different than what I was used to, the people were of assorted colors and when they saw me they sometimes stared, others turned away quickly telling their children to turn around. I felt an odd mixture of anxiety and frustration for I didnt know what to do except just stand and stare at this place. But in a way I felt proud for my world had always been happy but this world looked swamped with depression

Sample 4 (Word-Pair)

Word-pairs consist of sophisticated synonyms (e.g., *pride* and *pleasure*) and antonyms (e.g., *forlorn* and *happy*) as well as atypical pairs of words (e.g., *sibling rivalry* and *delight*). These require students to synthesize definitions of the words and to apply them creatively in an essay.

When the Word-Pair option is chosen, the teacher can use the word-pairs that are provided in Appendix B or make up a different word-pair. For this assignment, students are given two words such as *panic → secure* and are asked to write a story using these words, one that has a beginning, middle, and end. The story can be personal or it can be about someone they know or have read about. This a great exercise that helps students to think critically about how emotional situations transform and progress, and how the thoughts and feelings interact. Here is a sample essay using the word-pair *alienated → happy*.

"I felt *alienated* a few weeks ago when I found out about Andrew's birthday party and I hadn't received an invitation. I don't know why I didn't say anything to him because we are good friends. However, the day before the party my mom showed me the invitation that she misplaced. I became so *happy* because I really wanted to go to the party and I didn't think that Andrew would purposely not invite me. I wanted to scream at my mom though."

The Importance of Writing Short Essays

Good writing is a creative act that demands students approach the task as unique individuals who are willing to reveal their inner thoughts and feelings. If writing in school is to serve any realistic purpose, students should be encouraged to minimize imitative dialogue and maximize their own uniqueness. In doing so, students not only clarify their present reality, but more importantly, work towards becoming human beings who are capable of perceiving reality, not through the inordinate influences of others, but mostly through their own developed capacities.

When constructing essays, students are encouraged to write creatively by commingling any significant academic or social issue with original dialogue. In addition, the teacher should choose topics and introduce essays that commingle reality-based material and imagination as demonstrated in the three example essays. Personal essays are also encouraged. When incorporating their own ideas and personal experiences (versus copying information from a textbook) students gain more confidence in their own writing ability. Writing about personal experiences has also been shown to promote physical health, well-being and certain adaptive behaviors (Pennebaker, 1997).

Evaluating Essays

- Critique should never be negative. It is suggested that essays be graded as 'O' for O.K., 'G' for good, and 'T' for terrific.

- Essays should be evaluated on the basis of their creativity, content, and clarity, and whether or not the student stayed connected to the assigned task.

- Teachers should not spend a great deal of time analyzing errors. It is suggested that the teacher make a list of the most frequent errors (recurring patterns) and address the entire class instead of "red" marking each student's essay. This is in keeping with the overall philosophy of the program.

- Content and feeling are more important than analyzing errors.

- Each essay should only take 1 to 2 minutes to score.

Student Projects to Develop Emotional Literacy

Student Projects:
Special assignments to promote social
and emotional intelligence

In addition to the **6 Steps**, eight specific projects have been identified to promote social and emotional intelligence. Each project is designed to hone in on the skills associated with *Emotional Literacy*. The projects require students to write about or perform an activity pertaining to the perception of emotion, the use of emotion, the understanding of emotion, and the regulation of emotion in themselves and others. We recommend teachers wait about one month before assigning these projects - that way students are well-acquainted with the purpose of the program. In order to get through all the activities, teachers should assign one project every month. Finally, we encourage teachers to modify the projects to accommodate the needs of their grade level curriculum content as well as the needs of the students. Students should be provided with written guidelines for each project.

#	PROJECT	AREAS OF EMOTIONAL LITERACY
1	Collage or Mobile Project	Expression and Perception of Emotion
2	Anger Project	Self-and other awareness, Expression, Perception, Understanding, and Regulation of Emotion
3	Commercial Project	Expression, Perception, and Understanding Emotion
4	Sadness Project	Self-and other awareness, Expression, Perception, Use, Understanding, and Regulation of Emotion
5	Television Observation Project	Expression, Perception, Understanding, and Regulation of Emotion
6	Happiness Project	Self-and other awareness, Expression, Perception, Use, Understanding, and Regulation of Emotion
7	Art Appreciation Project	Expression, Perception, Use and Understanding of Emotion
8	Song Appreciation Project	Expression, Perception, Use and Understanding of Emotion

Project 1:
Collage or Mobile

The purpose of this project is for students to examine various facial expressions that depict emotions.

Perusing the newspaper, comic strips, and magazines are great ways for students to examine people's facial expressions. Students can easily find pictures of basic emotions such as anger, sadness, and happiness. With a little effort, they can also find complex emotional expressions such as pride, shame, guilt, and grief.

Activity:

Students create either a collage or mobile. The directions are simple and flexible. Students can work individually or in small groups. This is also a good assignment to incorporate the jigsaw classroom technique, which breaks students into small groups in which they each work on, and then present, a piece of critical information necessary so all students can get a complete grasp of the lesson.

1. The teacher decides to have students
   a. look for pictures pertaining to the expression of one emotion (e.g., happiness or anger),
   b. look for pictures that show a wide range of expressions of one emotion (e.g., annoyed to anger to furious), or
   c. look for pictures to express a lot of different emotions.
2. Students cut out the pictures from the magazines, comic strips, or newspaper.
3. Students then design a collage or a mobile.
4. The projects are usually collected and displayed in the classroom.
5. Students can also present their work to the class.

Project 2:
Self-Regulation — Anger

The purpose of this project is for students to explore in detail their own and others' feelings of anger and the different ways that people regulate anger.

Anger is activated by a feeling of frustration or of being restrained from the pursuit of a goal. We are most likely to get angry with someone when we believe we have suffered unjustified or intentional insult or injury. Research shows that expressing hostile anger often increases the anger, and may lead to ill health and problems in interpersonal relationships. Therefore, understanding why we get angry and learning effective ways of handling our anger is very important.

Activity I:
Students are asked to think about a time when they were really angry and then write a full story about the event. They must write about: (a) what made them angry, (b) how they initially handled the feeling, and (c) what the end result was. The story must have a beginning, middle, and end. Once the writing portion is complete, students then answer the following questions:

1. Why did that particular situation make you feel angry?
2. Think about what you did to handle your anger.
   a. Describe how you felt in detail. What kinds of thoughts and feelings did you have?
   b. How did you react? What exactly did you do?
   c. Did you have any physical symptoms? That is, how did your body react?
   d. How long did you remain angry?
   e. How long did it take before you felt better?
   f. What did you do to feel better? What eventually helped you to feel better?
   g. Did anyone help you to feel better? Who? How?

Activity II:
Students compare what makes them feel angry to what makes their friends and family members feel angry. This can be done in class or for homework.

1. Students answer the following questions about themselves:
   a. In general, what kinds of things make you feel angry?
   b. In general, how do you react when you get angry? That is, what do you do?
   c. In general, what do you do to help yourself feel better when you are angry?
2. Students interview 3 friends or 3 family members (no names are needed)
   a. Students ask these individuals to discuss 2 things that make them feel angry.
   b. They then ask them how they usually react when they get angry.
   c. They then ask them to describe 2 things that they usually do to help them feel better.

3. For the final part of the assignment, students compare and contrast what makes them feel angry from what makes their friends/family feel angry. They then answer these questions:
   a. What are the similarities and differences between what makes you feel angry and what makes your friend/family member angry?
   b. What are the similarities and differences between what you do and your friend/family members do when they get angry?
   c. What are the similarities and differences between the strategies that you use to handle your anger and the ways your friends/family members do?
   d. What were the most effective strategies that either you or your friends/family members used? Why were these the most effective strategies?

Project 3:
Analysis of a Commercial

The purpose of this project is for students to explore how television commercials influence thoughts and feelings.

Commercials are designed to manipulate us to think and feel a particular way about ourselves or a consumable product. Because of this, they provide a great medium to study emotions. The following classroom activity requires students to analyze the emotional content of a television commercial. Students can work individually or in small groups.

Activity I:
1. The teacher gives a five-minute introduction on how advertisers often play on our emotions to get our attention. Many commercials, for example, link their products with positive emotions like happiness by showing images of happy people using their products.
2. The teacher gives two examples of well-known commercials that play on our emotions. Example: Trident gum commercials promote and evoke happiness.

The teacher then asks students to think about the emotions or emotional triggers that commercials use, and share them with the class. Examples of emotions/emotional triggers include humor, fear, envy, loneliness, longing, violence, excitement, and worry. If the student gives an incomplete answer, the teacher should ask leading questions such as: What emotion does this trigger? How did the advertiser elicit this response? Who is the audience?

Activity II:
The teacher brings in a videotape of two or three commercials and shows them to the class. After the tape has been viewed, the teacher asks students questions about the commercials and the emotions that were elicited.

Examples: What emotions did the actors show? Who were they trying to influence? How could you tell? How did this commercial make you feel?

Activity III:
Students are put in small groups and each group is given a product to market. Students are asked to devise an advertising strategy (commercial idea) that involves an emotion. For example, if students are selling an alarm system, they might use the emotion of fear. They can include the target (kids, adults, teenagers, senior citizens), possible music that would help influence the targets, and the specific messages that the advertisers were trying to get across. Each group then shares the advertising strategy with the class, while the other class members analyze its emotional content.

Project 4:
Self-Regulation – Sadness

The purpose of this project is for students to explore in detail their own and others' feelings of sadness and the different ways that people regulate sad feelings.

Sadness is a relatively mild and brief emotion. Some of the typical causes of sadness are making mistakes, doing something to hurt others, or being forced to do something against your will. Sadness, however, can have an adaptive function. It can encourage us to change our lives. If, for example, we feel sad that we hurt another person, our sadness may motivate us to make amends. Sadness can also be a cue for other people to help us.

Activity I:
Students are asked to think about a time when they were really sad and write a full story about the event. They should write about what made them sad, how they initially handled the feeling, and what the end result was. The story must have a beginning, middle, and end. Students then answer the following questions.

1. Why did that particular situation make you feel sad?
2. Now, think about what you did to handle your sadness
   a. Describe how you felt in detail. What kinds of thoughts and feelings did you have?
   b. How did you react? What exactly did you do?
   c. Did you have any physical symptoms? That is, how did your body react?
   d. How long did you remain sad for?
   e. How long did it take before you felt better?
   f. What did you do to help yourself feel better? What eventually helped you to feel better?
   g. Did anyone help you to feel better? Who? How?

Activity II:
Students compare what makes them feel sad with what makes their friends and family members feel sad. This can be done in class or for homework.

1. Students answer the following questions about themselves:
   a. In general, what kinds of things make you feel sad?
   b. In general, how do you react when you get sad? That is, what do you do?
   c. In general, what do you do to help yourself feel better when you are sad?
2. Students interview 2 friends or 2 family members (no names are needed)
   a. Students ask these individuals to discuss 2 things that make them feel sad.
   b. They then ask them how they usually react when they get sad?
   c. They then ask them to describe 2 things that they usually do to help them to feel better.

3. For the final part of the assignment, students compare and contrast what makes them feel sad from what makes their friends feel sad. They then answer the following questions:
   a. What are the similarities and differences between what makes you feel sad and what makes your friend/family member sad?
   b. What are the similarities and differences between what you do and your friend/family members do when they get sad?
   c. What are the similarities and differences between the strategies that you use to handle your sadness and the ways your friends/family members do?
   d. What were the most effective strategies that either you or your friends/family members used? Why were these the most effective strategies?

Project 5:
Television Observation Project

The purpose of this project is for students to watch in detail and record the various emotions of a character on a television show.

The following activity requires students to analyze an actor on a sitcom. Actors on television shows, like people in everyday life, invariably express multiple emotions when interacting with others. Observing how actors express and regulate their emotions is a fun way to help students learn about emotions. The project is usually assigned as an at-home project.

Activity:
1. Choose a sitcom that would be enjoyable to watch. Record the show.
2. Pick one character on the television show that would be interesting to observe. The assignment is to watch how the person displays his or her emotions in one episode.
3. First, describe this person in one paragraph. What is the person's character like?
4. Now examine the person in detail on the show:
   a. Watch how they behave alone and with others (e.g., parents, friends, siblings, boss, co-workers, etc.).
   b. Pay particular attention to how the person acts in different contexts: home, school, work, play, etc.
   - What kinds of emotions did the person display?
   - Does this person have lots of different facial expressions in the show? Does this person express many different feelings or emotions in the episode?
   - Does this person have to handle any difficult situations in the show? If so, does the person handle them well? Explain.
   - Write down whatever you see that describes the person's emotions.

Project 6:
Happiness in Everyday Life

The purpose of this project is for students to examine how they and others manage positive emotions and maintain feelings of happiness.

When we refer to self-regulation, we normally think about changing our negative moods into positive moods, or recovering from an event that made us sad or angry. However, maintaining positive moods is also important. This project requires students to think about events that involve feeling happy and about strategies they have used to stay happy. Happiness is the feeling of joy, or at least contentment that something is right.

The project on happiness can be done at home or as a class activity in small groups, with or without presentations. Teachers can require students to do all of the following activities or select just one or two.

Activity I – The Happy Person:
1. How can we tell when someone is happy?
2. What's the difference between people you know who are generally happy versus people you know who are generally unhappy?
3. Think of someone you know who is generally happy. Describe that person. List at least 7 things that tell you the person is generally, happy. That is, what behaviors or actions does the person demonstrate that let you know he or she is happy? What makes this person unique?

Activity II – Enjoying Your Own Happiness:
1. What was your favorite celebration? Describe the celebration in detail. What happened?
2. Why was this celebration so great?
3. Who enjoyed it with you?

Activity III - Fun with Friends and Family:
1. Think of something you've done with a friend or family member that was really fun. Describe the event in detail. Who were you with?
2. Why was this activity so much fun?
3. Would you recommend others to do the same thing?
4. How often do you get to do this activity? How does it feel to think about this activity? What kinds of memories does it bring up?

Activity IV —Enjoying Other People's Happiness:

1. What is the nicest thing you have done for someone else (friend or family member)? Describe what you did in detail.

2. How did the person respond to what you did? Try to remember how they expressed their feelings.

3. In turn, how did you respond? How did it make you feel to see this person happy?

Project 7:
Art Appreciation Project

The purpose of this project is for students to become acutely aware of the display of emotions in art.

Artists create sculptures, paintings, and other fine art, which usually convey various emotions. Sometimes the emotions a piece of art conveys are obvious, sometimes not. Because we can never get into the head of the artist, we never know exactly what the artist was feeling when creating his or her art; nor do we know the message (if any) the artist was trying to convey in the piece of art. Therefore, in this project, there are no right or wrong answers.

For this project, students will be examining pieces of art and describing the emotions that the art conveys to them. This project starts off with an in-class activity, is followed by a homework assignment, and then culminates with an optional class presentation.

Activity I:
Bring several books of art to class and allow the students to look through them. These books can come from your own collection or from the library. Then spend five minutes discussing how art can make people feel certain emotions and how artists may feel certain emotions when creating art. For example, we often associate certain colors with emotion. (e.g., red = anger). Choose one painting and show it to the students. Ask them how it makes them feel and why it makes them feel that way? Ask them to be specific. Is it the landscaping? Is it the facial expressions? What's the general mood of the painting? This can also be a good occasion to see if there is consensus in the class. If there isn't consensus, then that can lead to a good conversation: art is subjective. Can we ever know what the artist was thinking/feeling when creating the piece of art?

Activity II:
Ask students to repeat this activity at home, on their own. Each student goes home and picks a piece of art. The art can be something displayed in the student's home (students should take a picture of it) or it can be from an art book, etc. If they don't have art books at home, provide students with art books from the school library. (If you think students might not have access to books of art, then the activity can also be done in class).

For homework, students should write a paragraph about how the painting made them feel. What was it about the painting that made them feel this way? Did the colors of the painting influence their perceptions?

The assignment can culminate in a show-and-tell of the art piece and a small presentation.

Project 8:
Music Appreciation Project

The purpose of this project is to help students recognize the emotional content of music.

Songwriters and singers create and perform music that expresses certain emotions. Sometimes the emotional content in a song is obvious and at other times the emotions in a song are communicated in subtle ways. Similar to the Art Project, there are no right or wrong answers to the Song Project; the only goal is for students to explore in detail the emotions that are evoked in a song they enjoy.

Activity:
1. Students identify a song that they enjoy listening to or a song that evokes a particular emotion they are interested in exploring. They can either record the song or they may already own the CD. Students should be cautioned not to bring in songs with inappropriate lyrics. First, students answer the following questions.
   a. What is the title of the song?
   b. Is the title reflecting an emotion?
2. Students are then instructed to think about the lyrics (words) to the song.
   a. What do you think the artist/band felt when writing this song?
   b. What kinds of words were used to indicate this feeling?
3. Students are then instructed to think about the sound of the music (instruments, etc.).
   a. What kind of feeling does the melody of the song express and why?
   b. Is the melody fast or slow? What does that indicate?
   c. What kinds of instruments are used in the song? Do they influence the "feeling" of the song?
4. Finally, they are asked how the song makes them feel and why?
5. The assignment can culminate in a small presentation in which students play the song for the class and discuss their answers to the questions.

Sample Lesson Plans for First Three Feeling Words

"What's on your mind?"
Lesson 1: _Elated_
Lesson 2: _Alienation_
Lesson 3: _Commitment_

"What's on your mind?"

·To introduce students to *Emotional Literacy*, a simple Self-Awareness activity can be done on or before the first instructional day. Because Self-Awareness (and awareness of others) is central to *Emotional Literacy*, this activity can also be employed at salient junctures during any instructional day. For example, if the class appears out of control, this activity can be done to settle everyone down and get them in touch with their feelings. We now know that children who lack self-awareness have difficulty controlling themselves, making appropriate decisions, and communicating their feelings. On the other hand, children with high self-awareness have better concentration and listening skills, which helps with academic performance and socialization (Elias et al., 1997).

Activity:
1. Teachers have students write down on a piece of paper any word or phrase that comes to mind, which describes how they are feeling at the current moment.
2. Teachers ask students to volunteer their responses and explain why they chose to write down that particular feeling or phrase.
   a. For example, one student may share that he is feeling nervous because of an upcoming test and another student may share that she is excited about an upcoming sports event.
3. A small class discussion then takes place. For example, students may volunteer similar thoughts and feelings, or the teacher can ask other students if they have similar thoughts and feelings. The discussion can focus on (but not be limited to) the idea that students have similar (and different) thoughts and feelings about many life events. In turn, students see that their peers share many of their thoughts and feelings. The activity also creates an atmosphere of equality and togetherness within the classroom.

Sample Lesson 1:
Elated

Step 1: Introducing the word *Elated*

A. Teacher poses the following question to class (in own way):
"What are some of the most exciting times you've had?"

B. Students and teacher share anecdotes
If students are hesitant, the teacher should share an anecdote.

C. Teacher introduces the word (in own way) after students demonstrate understanding of the term:
There is a (fancy) word that describes what we've been talking about. The word is *elated*. The word *elated* means to be or feel excited.

D. Definition is written on blackboard and students copy the word *elated* and its definition onto their worksheets.

Key Points: (a) Question, (b) Anecdote, (c) Introduction of Term

Step 1 is always done with **Step 2** on the first instructional day.

When students respond anecdotally it is natural for teachers to reply. For example, if a student speaks of having been separated from whatever or whomever, teacher would react sympathetically: "It must have felt really bad being left out, etc." It can also include a mini-conversation. Furthermore, it is a good policy to repeat part of the student response (as noted above) during the exchange. It tells the student that you really care and are listening to him or her. This same procedure applies to **Step 4**, the *Personal/Family Associations*. Additionally, this concept is important to any student's personal comment – in or out of context.

Step 2: *Design* and *Personified Explanation*

A. Teacher draws *Design* for the word *Elated* on blackboard.

B. Discussion: (Teacher states in own way): Now that you know the definition of the word *elated*, can anyone describe in his or her own words how this design looks like the word *elated*? (Students will come up with a variety of responses with or without using the word). When the teacher feels a reasonable understanding of the relationship between the word and the *Design* has been demonstrated (i.e., students have described *why* or *because* the *Design* looks like the word), the *PE* is written on the blackboard.

- If students are hesitant introduce the *PE* immediately.

C. Teacher writes *Personified Explanation* on the blackboard

D. Students write the *Personified Explanation* on their worksheets in the space provided under the *Design*.

"All of the circles are *elated* because they all won the game."

Key point: **Step 2** is always introduced immediately after **Step 1**.

Step 3: *Real World Associations (RWA)*

Step 3 (along with **Step 4**) is explained on Day 2. After the first three lessons, however, both **Steps 3 & 4** are completed for homework.

Design and *Personified Explanation* are left on the blackboard.

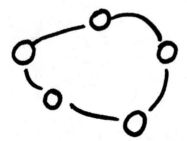

A. Teacher poses the following question to class (in own way):
In what way does the *Design* and *PE* relate to the "Real World?" What I mean is, think about what we've been discussing and learning in class (e.g., History or Literature) and try to come up with a statement using the word *elated*. Teacher should stress that any academic subject or important social issue can be employed. Students may also share something they feel strongly about.
- If students are hesitant teacher should help them construct a statement and then introduce our *RWA* below.

B. Teacher writes our example _RWA_ on the blackboard after a reasonable understanding of the _RWA_ has been demonstrated by the class.
(Teacher may use our example or one from the class, the more the better).
"Julius Caesar was _elated_ when he became a member of the Roman Oligarchy because he was able to help the poor Romans live a better lifestyle."

C. Students then write the _RWA_ on their worksheets and diagram it using the original _Design_.
Teacher shows students how to substitute the real people, places or things for the geometric symbols in the _Design_.

Step 4: _The Personal/Family Associations (PFA)_

Step 4 (along with **Step 3**) is explained on Instructional Day 2. After the first three lessons, however, this step is completed for homework.

A. The objective of _PFA_ is to have students make the connection between the new feeling word and personal experiences.

The _PFA_ is completed for homework. However, for the first 3 lessons students should be placed in small "family" groups. Students can take turns practicing with their school family. The teacher may assist students with the dialogue. Or, a sample family can model the process for the rest of the class.

B. Role Playing
Assign roles to students (e.g., mother(s), father(s), student(s))

Student states:
"I learned a new word in school today, the word is _elated._"
"When have you been _elated_?"

PFA's should include how, why, when or because...

C. Students then write about their own or family member's (real family member after the first three lessons) personal experience.
(Refer to **Step 4** for complete instructions on the homework assignment).

Example *PFA*
"I was *elated* when I was elected to be the class president."

     or a mother might state,

"Remember the other day when your father gave me the ring I always wanted? Well, that made me feel *elated*."

Step 5: *Classroom Discussions*

For the first 3 lessons, discussions take place on the third instructional day (after **Steps 3 & 4** have been introduced). After the first 3 lessons, discussions take place on the second instructional day after Steps **3 & 4** have been completed for homework.

The discussions are initiated by having students share either the *RWA* or *PFA* with the class. However, for the first 3 lessons the *Classroom Discussion* should take place in class on the third instructional day. Students take out their worksheets and refer to **Steps 3 & 4.**

A. Sharing of *RWA* or *PFA.*

Example Real World Association:
"Julius Caesar was *elated* when he became a member of the Roman Oligarchy because he was able to help the poor Romans live a better lifestyle."

B. Teacher initiates discussion with questions.
The teacher then asks questions, such as..."Why is it important to help people whenever we can? Why do you think Julius became *elated* after helping the poor Romans? When people who are in need of help receive it, how do you think they feel? Has anyone here ever helped someone who really needed help? Can you tell us about it?"
(The teacher determines the duration of the classroom discussion.)

Step 6: Creative Writing Assignment

• Refer to **Step 6** in the book.

Sample Lesson 2:
Alienation

Step 1: Introducing the word *Alienation*

A. Teacher poses the following question to class (in own way):
"How would you or anyone feel if he or she were left out of something - like not being invited to a party or not making the sports team?"

B. Students and teacher share anecdotes
If students are hesitant, the teacher should share an anecdote. Teacher anecdotes are always appropriate in addition to the students.

C. Teacher introduces the word (in own way) after students demonstrate understanding of the term:
"There is a (fancy) word that describes what we've been talking about. The word is *alienation.* The word *alienation* means to be or feel separated from something or someone."

D. Definition is written on blackboard and students copy the word *alienation* and its definition onto their worksheets.

Key Points: (a) Question, (b) Anecdote, (c) Introduction of Term

Step 1 is always done with **Step 2** on the first instructional day.

Step 2: *Design* and *Personified Explanation*

A. Teacher draws *Design* for the word *Alienation* on blackboard.

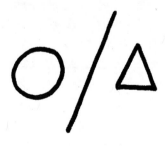

B. Discussion: (Teacher states in own way): Now that you know the definition of the word *alienation*, can anyone describe in his or her own words how this *Design* looks like the word *alienation*? (Students will come up with a variety of responses with or without using the word). When the teacher feels a reasonable understanding of the relationship between the word and the *Design* has been demonstrated (i.e., students have described *why* or *because* the *Design* looks like the word), the *PE* is written on the blackboard.

- If students are hesitant introduce the *PE* immediately.

<u>C. Teacher writes *Personified Explanation* on the blackboard</u>
Students write the *Personified Explanation* on their worksheets in the space provided under the *Design*.

"The circle is *alienated* from the triangle by the line."

Key point: **Step 2** is always introduced immediately after **Step 1**.

Step 3: *Real World Association (RWA)*

Step 3 (along with **Step 4**) is explained on Day 2. After the first three lessons, however, both **Steps 3 & 4** are completed for homework.

Design and *Personified Explanation* are left on the blackboard.

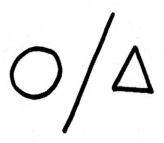

<u>A. Teacher poses the following question to class (in own way):</u>
In what way does the *Design* and *PE* relate to the "Real World?" What I mean is, think about what we've been discussing and learning in class (e.g., History or Literature) and try to come up with a statement using the word *alienation*. Teacher should stress that any academic subject or important social issue can be employed. Students may also share something they feel strongly about.
- If students are hesitant teacher should help them construct a statement and then introduce our *RWA* below.

<u>B. Teacher writes our example *RWA* on the blackboard after a reasonable</u> understanding of the *RWA* has been demonstrated by the class.
(Teacher may use our example or one from the class, the more the better).
"Students with disabilities often feel *alienated* from their peers because they can't participate in regular physical activities."

C. Students then write the *RWA* on their worksheets and diagram it using the original *Design.*

Teacher shows students how to substitute the real people, places or things for the geometric symbols in the *Design.*

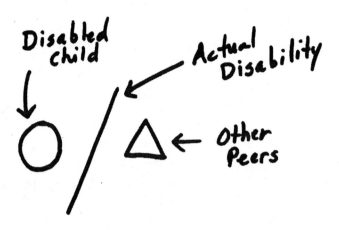

Step 4: *The Personal/Family Association (PFA)*

Step 4 (along with **Step 3**) is explained on Instructional Day 2. After the first three lessons, however, this step is completed for homework.

A. The objective of *PFA* is to have students make the connection between the new feeling word and personal experiences.

The *PFA* is completed for homework. However, for the first 3 lessons students should be placed in small "family" groups. Students can take turns practicing with their school family. The teacher may assist students with the dialogue. Or, a sample family can model the process for the rest of the class.

B. Role Playing
Assign roles to students (e.g., mother(s), father(s), student(s))

Student states:
"I learned a new word in school today, the word is *alienation.*"
"Have you ever felt *alienated?*"

PFA's should include how, why, when or because...

C. Students then write about their own or family member's (real family member after the first three lessons) personal experience.
(Refer to **Step 4** for complete instructions on the homework assignment).

Example *PFA*

"I was *alienated* from my friends when they didn't invite me to go for ice cream. I felt really lonely and sad."

or a father might state,

"Son, when I was in middle school I felt *alienated* because I was too small to be on the football team."

Step 5: *Classroom Discussions*

For the first 3 lessons, discussions take place on the third instructional day (after **Steps 3 & 4** have been introduced). After the first 3 lessons, discussions take place on the second instructional day after **Steps 3 & 4** have been completed for homework.

The discussions are initiated by having students share either the *RWA* or *PFA* with the class. However, for the first 3 lessons the *Classroom Discussion* should take place in class on the third instructional day. Students take out their worksheets and refer to **Steps 3 & 4**.

A. Sharing of *RWA* or *PFA*.

Example Real World Association:
"Children with disabilities often feel *alienated* because they can't participate in regular physical activities."

B. Teacher initiates discussion with questions.
The teacher then asks questions, such as...How do you feel about disabled students being *alienated* from social activities? What can we all do to help someone like this become more actively involved with different activities? Has anyone here ever had a friend who was disabled? Can you tell us about it? What can we as individuals do to help make a disabled child feel better about him/her self. How can we show our concern for his or her feelings of *alienation*? (The teacher determines the duration of the *Classroom Discussion*.)

Step 6: Creative Writing Assignment

- Refer to **Step 6** in the book.

Sample Lesson 3:
Commitment

Step 1: Introducing the word *Commitment*

A. Teacher poses the following question to class (in own way):
"What are some very important pledges or promises that we make in our lives?"

B. Students and Teacher share anecdotes
If students are hesitant, the teacher should share an anecdote.

C. Teacher introduces the word (in own way) after students demonstrate understanding of the term:
There is a (fancy) word that describes what we've been talking about. The word is *commitment*. The word *commitment* means to pledge or promise.

D. Definition is written on blackboard and students copy the word *commitment* and its definition onto their worksheets.

Step 2: *Design* and *Personified Explanation*

A. Teacher draws *Design* for the word *Commitment* on blackboard.

B. Discussion: (Teacher states in own way): Now that you know the definition of the word *commitment*, can anyone describe in his or her own words how this *Design* looks like the word *commitment*? (Students will come up with a variety of responses with or without using the word). When the teacher feels a reasonable understanding of the relationship between the word and the *Design* has been demonstrated (i.e., students have described *why* or *because* the design looks like the word), the *PE* is written on the blackboard.

• If students are hesitant introduce the *PE* immediately.

C. Teacher writes _Personified Explanation_ on the blackboard

D. Students write the _Personified Explanation_ on their worksheets in the space provided under the _Design._

The _Design_ looks like the word _commitment_ because the line will go in any direction to achieve its goal.

Key point: **Step 2** is always introduced immediately after **Step 1**.

Step 3: _Real World Association (RWA)_

Step 3 (along with **Step 4**) is explained on Day 2. After the first three lessons, however, both **Steps 3 & 4** are completed for homework.

Design and _Personified Explanation_ are left on the blackboard.

A. Teacher poses the following question to class (in own way):
In what way does the _Design_ and _PE_ relate to the "Real World?" What I mean is, think about what we've been discussing and learning in class (e.g., History or Literature) and try to come up with a statement using the word _commitment._ Teacher should stress that any academic subject or important social issue can be employed. Students may also share something they feel strongly about.
  • If students are hesitant teacher should help them construct a statement and then introduce our _RWA_ below.

B. Teacher writes our example _RWA_ on the blackboard after a reasonable understanding of the _RWA_ has been demonstrated by the class.
(Teacher may use our example or one from the class, the more the better).
"In the Lion King, Simba was _committed_ to returning to his village because he wanted to insure the future of the Pride (the other lions)."

C. Students then write the _RWA_ on their worksheets and diagram it using the original _Design._
Teacher shows students how to substitute the real people, places or things for the geometric symbols in the _Design._ As can be seen, some _Designs_ can be diagrammed with simple statements

Simba on his journey

Step 4: *The Personal/Family Association (PFA)*

Step 4 (along with **Step 3**) is explained on Instructional Day 2. After the first three lessons, however, this step is completed for homework.

A. The objective of *PFA* is to have students make the connection between the new feeling word and personal experiences.

The *PFA* is completed for homework. However, for the first 3 lessons students should be placed in small "family" groups. Students can take turns practicing with their school family. The teacher may assist students with the dialogue. Or, a sample family can model the process for the rest of the class.

B. Role Playing
Assign roles to students (e.g., mother(s), father(s), student(s))

Student states:
"I learned a new word in school today, the word is *commitment*."
"Have you ever been *committed* to doing anything?"

PFA's should include how, why, when or because...

C. Students then write about their own or family member's (real family member after the first three lessons) personal experience).
(Refer to **Step 4** for complete instructions on the homework assignment).

Example *PFA*:
"I am *committed* to my karate class because I want to get a black belt."

       or, an older sibling might state

"I really *committed* to practicing hockey because I want our team to come in first place this year."

Step 5: *Classroom Discussions*

For the first 3 lessons, discussions take place on the third instructional day (after **Steps 3 & 4** have been introduced). After the first 3 lessons, discussions take place on the second instructional day after **Steps 3 & 4** have been completed for homework.

The discussions are initiated by having students share either the *RWA* or *PFA* with the class. However, for the first 3 lessons the *Classroom Discussion* should take place in class on the third instructional day. Students take out their worksheets and refer to **Steps 3 & 4**.

A. Sharing of *RWA* or *PFA*.

Example Real World Association:
"In the Lion King, Simba was *committed* to returning to his village because he wanted to insure the future of the Pride (the other lions)."

B. Teacher initiates discussion with questions.

The teacher then asks questions, such as...Why do you think Simba was so *committed* to helping the Pride? How do you think the members of the Pride felt about Simba? Has anyone here ever been *committed* to anything? Can you tell us about it? Why do some people *commit* themselves to achieving their goals or helping others, and other people make very few or even no *commitments?* (The teacher determines the duration of the *Classroom Discussion*.)

Step 6: Creative Writing Assignment

• Refer to **Step 6** in the book.

Program Materials:
Teacher Lesson Sheets and
Student Worksheets

Teacher Lesson Sheet

Elated - *to be or feel excited*

Step 1: Question
What are some of the most exciting times you've had?

Word Introduction: *The word **elated** means to be or feel excited.*

Step 2: *Design*

Personified Explanation (PE): *All of the circles are **elated** because they all won the game.*

Step 3: *Real World Association (RWA)*

In what way does the *Design* and *PE* relate to the "Real World?" Write one or more sentences relating the word ***elated*** to something you've learned in class, a news story, a social event, or anything you feel strongly about. Substitute the symbols in the *Design* for the real people/places/things in your *RWA*.

_____

_____

_____

Now, diagram your *RWA* using key words from the *RWA* or other words of your choice.

Step 4: Personal/Family Association (PFA)

Write one or more sentences relating the word ***elated*** to your own personal experience or the personal experience of someone important in your life (e.g., parent, sibling, friend). Make sure the *PFA* expresses your own or chosen others' feelings.

_____

_____

_____

Student Worksheet

Step 1: Question

_____
Feeling Word

What are some of the most exciting times you've had?

Definition: _____

_____

Step 2: *Design*

Personified Explanation (PE): _____

_____

Step 3: *Real World Association (RWA)*

In what way does the *Design* and PE relate to the "Real World?" Write one or more sentences relating the word _____ to something you've learned in class, a news story, a social event, or anything you feel strongly about. Substitute the symbols in the *Design* for the real people/places/things in your *RWA*.

_____

_____

Now, diagram your *RWA* using key words from the *RWA* or other words of your choice.

Step 4: *Personal/Family Association (PFA)*

Write one or more sentences relating the word _____ to your own personal experience or the personal experience of someone important in your life (e.g., parent, sibling, friend). Make sure the *PFA* expresses your own or chosen others' feelings.

_____

_____

_____

Teacher Lesson Sheet

Alienation - to be or feel separated from someone or something

Step 1: Question
When was the last time you (or someone you know) were left out of something you really wanted to participate in - like not being invited to a party or not making the sports team?
Word Introduction: *The word **alienation** means to be or feel separated from someone or something.*

Step 2: *Design*

Personified Explanation (PE): *The circle is **alienated** from the triangle by the line.*

Step 3: *Real World Association (RWA)*
In what way does the *Design* and *PE* relate to the "Real World?" Write one or more sentences relating the word ***alienation*** to something you've learned in class, a news story, a social event, or anything you feel strongly about. Substitute the symbols in the *Design* for the real people/places/things in your *RWA*.

_____

_____

_____

Now, diagram your *RWA* using key words from the *RWA* or other words of your choice.

Step 4: Personal/Family Association (PFA)
Write one or more sentences relating the word ***alienation*** to your own personal experience or the personal experience of someone important in your life (e.g., parent, sibling, friend). Make sure the *PFA* expresses your own or chosen others' feelings.

_____

_____

_____

Student Worksheet

Step 1: Question

Feeling Word

When was the last time you (or someone you know) were left out of something you really wanted to participate in - like not being invited to a party or not making the sports team?

Definition: _____

_____

Step 2: *Design*

Personified Explanation (PE): _____

_____

Step 3: *Real World Association (RWA)*

In what way does the *Design* and PE relate to the "Real World?" Write one or more sentences relating the word _____ to something you've learned in class, a news story, a social event, or anything you feel strongly about. Substitute the symbols in the *Design* for the real people/places/things in your *RWA*.

_____

_____

_____

Now, diagram your *RWA* using key words from the *RWA* or other words of your choice.

Step 4: *Personal/Family Association (PFA)*

Write one or more sentences relating the word _____to your own personal experience or the personal experience of someone important in your life (e.g., parent, sibling, friend). Make sure the *PFA* expresses your own or chosen others' feelings.

_____

_____

_____

Teacher Lesson Sheet

Commitment - to make a pledge or promise to do something

Step 1: Question
What are some very important pledges or promises that we make in our lives?

Word Introduction: *The word **commitment** means to make a pledge or promise to do something.*

Step 2: *Design*

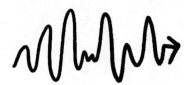

Personified Explanation (PE): *The Design looks like the word **commitment** because the line will go in any direction to achieve its goal.*

Step 3: *Real World Association (RWA)*
In what way does the *Design* and *PE* relate to the "Real World?" Write one or more sentences relating the word ***commitment*** to something you've learned in class, a news story, a social event, or anything you feel strongly about. Substitute the symbols in the *Design* for the real people/places/things in your *RWA*.

_____

_____

_____

Now, diagram your *RWA* using key words from the *RWA* or other words of your choice.

Step 4: Personal/Family Association (PFA)
Write one or more sentences relating the word ***commitment*** to your own personal experience or the personal experience of someone important in your life (e.g., parent, sibling, friend). Make sure the *PFA* expresses your own or chosen others' feelings.

_____

_____

_____

Student Worksheet

_____
Feeling Word

Step 1: Question

What are some very important pledges or promises that we make in our lives?

Definition: _____

_____

Step 2: *Design*

Personified Explanation (PE): _____

_____

Step 3: *Real World Association (RWA)*

In what way does the *Design* and PE relate to the "Real World?" Write one or more sentences relating the word _____ to something you've learned in class, a news story, a social event, or anything you feel strongly about. Substitute the symbols in the *Design* for the real people/places/things in your *RWA*.

_____

_____

_____

Now, diagram your *RWA* using key words from the *RWA* or other words of your choice.

Step 4: *Personal/Family Association (PFA)*

Write one or more sentences relating the word _____to your own personal experience or the personal experience of someone important in your life (e.g., parent, sibling, friend). Make sure the *PFA* expresses your own or chosen others' feelings.

_____

_____

_____

Teacher Lesson Sheet

Adapt - to adjust or fit in

Step 1: Question
What are some difficult situations you have had to adjust to - such as moving to a new area, meeting new friends or going to a new school?
Word Introduction: *The word **adapt** means to adjust or to fit in.*

Step 2: *Design*

Personified Explanation (PE): *The lone triangle is having difficulty **adapting** to its new environment because it doesn't recognize any of the other shapes.*

Step 3: *Real World Association (RWA)*

In what way does the *Design* and *PE* relate to the "Real World?" Write one or more sentences relating the word ***adapt*** to something you've learned in class, a news story, a social event, or anything you feel strongly about. Substitute the symbols in the *Design* for the real people/places/things in your *RWA*.

_____

_____

_____

Now, diagram your *RWA* using key words from the *RWA* or other words of your choice.

Step 4: Personal/Family Association (PFA)

Write one or more sentences relating the word ***adapt*** to your own personal experience or the personal experience of someone important in your life (e.g., parent, sibling, friend). Make sure the *PFA* expresses your own or chosen others' feelings.

_____

_____

_____

Student Worksheet

Step 1: Question

Feeling Word

What are some difficult situations you have had to adjust to - such as moving to a new area, meeting new friends or going to a new school?

Definition: _____

_____

Step 2: *Design*

Personified Explanation (PE): _____

_____

Step 3: *Real World Association (RWA)*

In what way does the *Design* and PE relate to the "Real World?" Write one or more sentences relating the word _____ to something you've learned in class, a news story, a social event, or anything you feel strongly about. Substitute the symbols in the *Design* for the real people/places/things in your *RWA*.

_____

_____

_____

Now, diagram your *RWA* using key words from the *RWA* or other words of your choice.

Step 4: *Personal/Family Association (PFA)*

Write one or more sentences relating the word _____ to your own personal experience or the personal experience of someone important in your life (e.g., parent, sibling, friend). Make sure the *PFA* expresses your own or chosen others' feelings.

_____

_____

_____

Teacher Lesson Sheet

Addiction - *an uncontrollable habit causing harm to one's self*

Step 1: Question
How does a person know when he or she is no longer in control of a bad habit - such as smoking or taking drugs?

Word Introduction: To have an **addiction** means to have an uncontrollable habit which causes harm to oneself.

Step 2: *Design*

*Personified Explanation (PE): This Design looks like the word **addiction** because the circle can't stop filling itself with the small poisonous dots.*

Step 3: *Real World Association (RWA)*

In what way does the *Design* and *PE* relate to the "Real World?" Write one or more sentences relating the word **addiction** to something you've learned in class, a news story, a social event, or anything you feel strongly about. Substitute the symbols in the *Design* for the real people/places/things in your *RWA*.

_____

_____

_____

Now, diagram your *RWA* using key words from the *RWA* or other words of your choice.

Step 4: Personal/Family Association (PFA)

Write one or more sentences relating the word **addiction** to your own personal experience or the personal experience of someone important in your life (e.g., parent, sibling, friend). Make sure the *PFA* expresses your own or chosen others' feelings.

_____

_____

_____

Student Worksheet

_____

Student name

Step 1: Question

_____

Feeling Word

How does a person know when he or she is no longer in control of a bad habit - such as smoking or taking drugs?

Definition: _____

_____

Step 2: _Design_

Personified Explanation (PE): _____

_____

Step 3: _Real World Association (RWA)_

In what way does the _Design_ and PE relate to the "Real World?" Write one or more sentences relating the word _____ to something you've learned in class, a news story, a social event, or anything you feel strongly about. Substitute the symbols in the _Design_ for the real people/places/things in your _RWA_.

_____

_____

_____

Now, diagram your _RWA_ using key words from the _RWA_ or other words of your choice.

Step 4: _Personal/Family Association (PFA)_

Write one or more sentences relating the word _____ to your own personal experience or the personal experience of someone important in your life (e.g., parent, sibling, friend). Make sure the _PFA_ expresses your own or chosen others' feelings.

_____

_____

_____

Teacher Lesson Sheet

Agony - *to experience great pain*

Step 1: Question
What was one of the most painful experiences you or someone you know ever had - such as a terrible accident, serious illness or personal disappointment?
Word Introduction: *The word **agony** means to experience great pain.*

Step 2: *Design*

Personified Explanation (PE): *The circle is in **agony** because it is constantly being attacked by the arrows.*

Step 3: *Real World Association (RWA)*
In what way does the *Design* and *PE* relate to the "Real World?" Write one or more sentences relating the word **agony** to something you've learned in class, a news story, a social event, or anything you feel strongly about. Substitute the symbols in the *Design* for the real people/places/things in your *RWA*.

_____

_____

_____

Now, diagram your *RWA* using key words from the *RWA* or other words of your choice.

Step 4: Personal/Family Association (PFA)
Write one or more sentences relating the word **agony** to your own personal experience or the personal experience of someone important in your life (e.g., parent, sibling, friend). Make sure the *PFA* expresses your own or chosen others' feelings.

_____

_____

_____

Student Worksheet

_____
Feeling Word

Step 1: Question
What was one of the most painful experiences you or someone you know ever had - such as a terrible accident, serious illness or personal disappointment?

Definition: _____

_____

Step 2: *Design*

Personified Explanation (PE): _____

_____

Step 3: *Real World Association (RWA)*
In what way does the *Design* and PE relate to the "Real World?" Write one or more sentences relating the word _____ to something you've learned in class, a news story, a social event, or anything you feel strongly about. Substitute the symbols in the *Design* for the real people/places/things in your *RWA*.

_____

_____

_____

Now, diagram your *RWA* using key words from the *RWA* or other words of your choice.

Step 4: *Personal/Family Association (PFA)*
Write one or more sentences relating the word _____to your own personal experience or the personal experience of someone important in your life (e.g., parent, sibling, friend). Make sure the *PFA* expresses your own or chosen others' feelings.

_____

_____

_____

Teacher Lesson Sheet

Altruism - *to give something without expecting anything in return*

Step 1: Question
What kind of person does things out of concern for others?

Word Introduction: *The word* **altruism** *means to give something without expecting anything in return.*

Step 2: *Design*

Personified Explanation (PE): *The big circle is being* **altruistic** *by protecting the small circle from the attacking arrows because it knows the small circle can't protect itself.*

Step 3: *Real World Association (RWA)*
In what way does the *Design* and *PE* relate to the "Real World?" Write one or more sentences relating the word ***altruistic*** to something you've learned in class, a news story, a social event, or anything you feel strongly about. Substitute the symbols in the *Design* for the real people/places/things in your *RWA*.

_____

_____

_____

Now, diagram your *RWA* using key words from the *RWA* or other words of your choice.

Step 4: *Personal/Family Association (PFA)*
Write one or more sentences relating the word ***altruistic*** to your own personal experience or the personal experience of someone important in your life (e.g., parent, sibling, friend). Make sure the *PFA* expresses your own or chosen others' feelings.

_____

_____

_____

Student Worksheet

Step 1: Question

Feeling Word

What kind of person does things out of concern for others?

Definition: _____

_____

Step 2: *Design*

Personified Explanation (PE): _____

_____

Step 3: *Real World Association (RWA)*

In what way does the *Design* and PE relate to the "Real World?" Write one or more sentences relating the word _____ to something you've learned in class, a news story, a social event, or anything you feel strongly about. Substitute the symbols in the *Design* for the real people/places/things in your *RWA*.

_____

_____

Now, diagram your *RWA* using key words from the *RWA* or other words of your choice.

Step 4: *Personal/Family Association (PFA)*

Write one or more sentences relating the word _____ to your own personal experience or the personal experience of someone important in your life (e.g., parent, sibling, friend). Make sure the *PFA* expresses your own or chosen others' feelings.

_____

_____

Teacher Lesson Sheet

Ambivalent - *to have mixed feelings*

Step 1: Question
Have you ever had mixed or confused feelings about something, like not knowing what you wanted for your birthday or whether or not you should talk to a friend about something that really bothers you?
Word Introduction: *To feel **ambivalent** is to have mixed or confused feelings about something.*

Step 2: *Design*

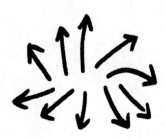

Personified Explanation (PE): *The arrows are **ambivalent** because they don't know which way to go to solve their problems.*

Step 3: *Real World Association (RWA)*
In what way does the *Design* and *PE* relate to the "Real World?" Write one or more sentences relating the word ***ambivalent*** to something you've learned in class, a news story, a social event, or anything you feel strongly about. Substitute the symbols in the *Design* for the real people/places/things in your *RWA.*

_____

_____

_____

Now, diagram your *RWA* using key words from the *RWA* or other words of your choice.

Step 4: Personal/Family Association (PFA)
Write one or more sentences relating the word ***ambivalent*** to your own personal experience or the personal experience of someone important in your life (e.g., parent, sibling, friend). Make sure the *PFA* expresses your own or chosen others' feelings.

_____

_____

_____

Student Worksheet

Student name

Feeling Word

Step 1: Question
Have you ever had mixed or confused feelings about something, like not knowing what you wanted for your birthday or whether or not you should talk to a friend about something that really bothers you?

Definition: _____

_____

Step 2: *Design*

Personified Explanation (PE): _____

_____

Step 3: *Real World Association (RWA)*
In what way does the *Design* and PE relate to the "Real World?" Write one or more sentences relating the word _____ to something you've learned in class, a news story, a social event, or anything you feel strongly about. Substitute the symbols in the *Design* for the real people/places/things in your *RWA*.

_____

_____

_____

Now, diagram your *RWA* using key words from the *RWA* or other words of your choice.

Step 4: *Personal/Family Association (PFA)*
Write one or more sentences relating the word _____ to your own personal experience or the personal experience of someone important in your life (e.g., parent, sibling, friend). Make sure the *PFA* expresses your own or chosen others' feelings.

_____

_____

_____

Teacher Lesson Sheet

Anxiety - *to worry a great deal*

Step 1: Question

What worries do you have? What are some fears or concerns that you have - such as passing a test or being chosen to be a member of some team or group?

Word Introduction: *The word* **anxiety** *means to worry or be overly concerned about something.*

Step 2: *Design*

Personified Explanation (PE): *The little circle is* **anxious** *because it thinks it will never be as big as close as the other circles.*

Step 3: *Real World Association (RWA)*

In what way does the *Design* and *PE* relate to the "Real World?" Write one or more sentences relating the word **anxious** to something you've learned in class, a news story, a social event, or anything you feel strongly about. Substitute the symbols in the *Design* for the real people/places/things in your *RWA*.

_____

_____

_____

Now, diagram your *RWA* using key words from the *RWA* or other words of your choice.

Step 4: Personal/Family Association (PFA)

Write one or more sentences relating the word **anxious** to your own personal experience or the personal experience of someone important in your life (e.g., parent, sibling, friend). Make sure the *PFA* expresses your own or chosen others' feelings.

_____

_____

_____

Student Worksheet

_____
Student name

_____
Feeling Word

Step 1: Question
What worries do you have? What are some fears or concerns that you have - such as passing a test or being chosen to be a member of some team or group?

Definition: _____

_____

Step 2: *Design*

Personified Explanation (PE): _____

_____

Step 3: *Real World Association (RWA)*
In what way does the *Design* and PE relate to the "Real World?" Write one or more sentences relating the word _____ to something you've learned in class, a news story, a social event, or anything you feel strongly about. Substitute the symbols in the *Design* for the real people/places/things in your *RWA*.

_____

_____

_____

Now, diagram your *RWA* using key words from the *RWA* or other words of your choice.

Step 4: *Personal/Family Association (PFA)*
Write one or more sentences relating the word _____ to your own personal experience or the personal experience of someone important in your life (e.g., parent, sibling, friend). Make sure the *PFA* expresses your own or chosen others' feelings.

_____

_____

_____

Teacher Lesson Sheet

Apprehension - *fear of something that may happen in the future*

Step 1: Question
What fears do you have about the future?

Word Introduction: *The word* **apprehension** *means to fear something that may happen in the future.*

Step 2: *Design*

Personified Explanation (PE): *The dot inside the circle is* **apprehensive** *about leaving the circle because it believes it will be hurt by the gang of dots.*

Step 3: *Real World Association (RWA)*

In what way does the *Design* and *PE* relate to the "Real World?" Write one or more sentences relating the word **apprehension** to something you've learned in class, a news story, a social event, or anything you feel strongly about. Substitute the symbols in the *Design* for the real people/places/things in your *RWA*.

_____

_____

_____

Now, diagram your *RWA* using key words from the *RWA* or other words of your choice.

Step 4: Personal/Family Association (PFA)

Write one or more sentences relating the word **apprehension** to your own personal experience or the personal experience of someone important in your life (e.g., parent, sibling, friend). Make sure the *PFA* expresses your own or chosen others' feelings.

_____

_____

_____

Student Worksheet

Step 1: Question

Feeling Word

What fears do you have about the future?

Definition: _____

_____

Step 2: *Design*

Personified Explanation (PE): _____

_____

Step 3: *Real World Association (RWA)*

In what way does the *Design* and PE relate to the "Real World?" Write one or more sentences relating the word _____ to something you've learned in class, a news story, a social event, or anything you feel strongly about. Substitute the symbols in the *Design* for the real people/places/things in your *RWA*.

_____

_____

_____

Now, diagram your *RWA* using key words from the *RWA* or other words of your choice.

Step 4: *Personal/Family Association (PFA)*

Write one or more sentences relating the word _____ to your own personal experience or the personal experience of someone important in your life (e.g., parent, sibling, friend). Make sure the *PFA* expresses your own or chosen others' feelings.

_____

_____

_____

Teacher Lesson Sheet

Arrogant - feeling superior and overly proud

Step 1: Question
Do you know someone who often shows off and tries to make a big impression on everyone? Why does he or she behave that way?
Word Introduction: *The word **arrogant** means to feel superior or overly proud.*

Step 2: *Design*

Personified Explanation (PE): *The big triangle is **arrogant** because it thinks it is tougher than the little triangles - just because it's bigger.*

Step 3: *Real World Association (RWA)*

In what way does the *Design* and *PE* relate to the "Real World?" Write one or more sentences relating the word **arrogant** to something you've learned in class, a news story, a social event, or anything you feel strongly about. Substitute the symbols in the *Design* for the real people/places/things in your *RWA*.

_____

_____

_____

Now, diagram your *RWA* using key words from the *RWA* or other words of your choice.

Step 4: Personal/Family Association (PFA)

Write one or more sentences relating the word **arrogant** to your own personal experience or the personal experience of someone important in your life (e.g., parent, sibling, friend). Make sure the *PFA* expresses your own or chosen others' feelings.

_____

_____

_____

Student Worksheet

Feeling Word

Step 1: Question
Do you know someone who often shows off and tries to make a big impression on everyone? Why does he or she behave that way?

Definition: _____

_____

Step 2: *Design*

△ ▲▲▲

Personified Explanation (PE): _____

_____

Step 3: *Real World Association (RWA)*
In what way does the *Design* and PE relate to the "Real World?" Write one or more sentences relating the word _____ to something you've learned in class, a news story, a social event, or anything you feel strongly about. Substitute the symbols in the *Design* for the real people/places/things in your *RWA*.

_____

_____

_____

Now, diagram your *RWA* using key words from the *RWA* or other words of your choice.

Step 4: *Personal/Family Association (PFA)*
Write one or more sentences relating the word _____ to your own personal experience or the personal experience of someone important in your life (e.g., parent, sibling, friend). Make sure the *PFA* expresses your own or chosen others' feelings.

_____

_____

_____

Teacher Lesson Sheet

Attitude - a person's thoughts and feelings about something

Step 1: Question
How does our frame of mind affect what we do and how well we do it?

Word Introduction: *A person's **attitude** is his or her thoughts and feelings about something.*

Step 2: *Design*

Personified Explanation (PE): *The arrow on the left has a positive **attitude** because it won't hang out with the other arrows that are negative.*

Step 3: *Real World Association (RWA)*

In what way does the *Design* and *PE* relate to the "Real World?" Write one or more sentences relating the word ***attitude*** to something you've learned in class, a news story, a social event, or anything you feel strongly about. Substitute the symbols in the *Design* for the real people/places/things in your *RWA*.

_____

_____

_____

Now, diagram your *RWA* using key words from the *RWA* or other words of your choice.

Step 4: Personal/Family Association (PFA)

Write one or more sentences relating the word ***attitude*** to your own personal experience or the personal experience of someone important in your life (e.g., parent, sibling, friend). Make sure the *PFA* expresses your own or chosen others' feelings.

_____

_____

_____

Student Worksheet

Step 1: Question

_____
Feeling Word

How does our frame of mind affect what we do and how well we do it?

Definition: _____

_____

Step 2: *Design*

Personified Explanation (PE): _____

_____

Step 3: *Real World Association (RWA)*
In what way does the *Design* and PE relate to the "Real World?" Write one or more
sentences relating the word _____ to something you've learned in class,
a news story, a social event, or anything you feel strongly about. Substitute the
symbols in the *Design* for the real people/places/things in your *RWA*.

_____

_____

Now, diagram your *RWA* using key words from the *RWA* or other words of your choice.

Step 4: *Personal/Family Association (PFA)*
Write one or more sentences relating the word _____to your own personal
experience or the personal experience of someone important in your life (e.g., parent,
sibling, friend). Make sure the *PFA* expresses your own or chosen others' feelings.

_____

_____

Teacher Lesson Sheet

Communicate - *to exchange ideas and information with others*

Step 1: Question

What is a major cause of most arguments? What is important in a good relationship?

Word Introduction: *To **communicate** is to exchange thoughts and feelings with others.*

Step 2: *Design*

Personified Explanation (PE): *Because the different shapes are **communicating** effectively, they are learning a lot about each other's similarities and differences.*

Step 3: *Real World Association (RWA)*

_____

_____

_____

Now, diagram your *RWA* using key words from the *RWA* or other words of your choice.

Step 4: *Personal/Family Association (PFA)*

_____

_____

_____

Student Worksheet

Step 1: Question

Feeling Word

What is a major cause of most arguments? What is important in a good relationship?

Definition: _____

_____

Step 2: *Design*

○ △ □

Personified Explanation (PE): _____

_____

Step 3: *Real World Association (RWA)*

In what way does the *Design* and PE relate to the "Real World?" Write one or more sentences relating the word _____ to something you've learned in class, a news story, a social event, or anything you feel strongly about. Substitute the symbols in the *Design* for the real people/places/things in your *RWA*.

_____

_____

_____

Now, diagram your *RWA* using key words from the *RWA* or other words of your choice.

Step 4: *Personal/Family Association (PFA)*

Write one or more sentences relating the word _____ to your own personal experience or the personal experience of someone important in your life (e.g., parent, sibling, friend). Make sure the *PFA* expresses your own or chosen others' feelings.

_____

_____

_____

Teacher Lesson Sheet

Compassion - to feel sorrow and sympathy for someone's misfortune

Step 1: Question
What kinds of feelings do you get when you hear about starving children or about someone with a serious illness?
Word Introduction: *The word **compassion** means to feel sorrow for someone's pain or misfortune.*

Step 2: *Design*

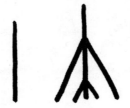

Personified Explanation (PE): *The line standing on its own feels **compassion** for the other line because it cannot stand on its own.*

Step 3: *Real World Association (RWA)*
In what way does the *Design* and *PE* relate to the "Real World?" Write one or more sentences relating the word ***compassion*** to something you've learned in class, a news story, a social event, or anything you feel strongly about. Substitute the symbols in the *Design* for the real people/places/things in your *RWA*.

_____

_____

_____

Now, diagram your *RWA* using key words from the *RWA* or other words of your choice.

Step 4: Personal/Family Association (PFA)
Write one or more sentences relating the word ***compassion*** to your own personal experience or the personal experience of someone important in your life (e.g., parent, sibling, friend). Make sure the *PFA* expresses your own or chosen others' feelings.

_____

_____

_____

Student Worksheet

Feeling Word

Step 1: Question

What kinds of feelings do you get when you hear about starving children or about someone with a serious illness?

Definition: _____

_____

Step 2: *Design*

Personified Explanation (PE): _____

_____

Step 3: *Real World Association (RWA)*

In what way does the *Design* and PE relate to the "Real World?" Write one or more sentences relating the word _____ to something you've learned in class, a news story, a social event, or anything you feel strongly about. Substitute the symbols in the *Design* for the real people/places/things in your *RWA*.

_____

_____

_____

Now, diagram your *RWA* using key words from the *RWA* or other words of your choice.

Step 4: *Personal/Family Association (PFA)*

Write one or more sentences relating the word _____to your own personal experience or the personal experience of someone important in your life (e.g., parent, sibling, friend). Make sure the *PFA* expresses your own or chosen others' feelings.

_____

_____

_____

Teacher Lesson Sheet

Compromise - *to settle something by giving something up*

Step 1: Question
Has anyone ever refused to do something and then finally agreed in order to be able to do what you wanted?
Word Introduction: *To **compromise** means to settle something by giving something up.*

Step 2: *Design*

Personified Explanation (PE): *The lone boxes refuse to **compromise** and play on the team with the other boxes because they can't be the co-captains of the team.*

Step 3: *Real World Association (RWA)*

In what way does the *Design* and *PE* relate to the "Real World?" Write one or more sentences relating the word ***compromise*** to something you've learned in class, a news story, a social event, or anything you feel strongly about. Substitute the symbols in the *Design* for the real people/places/things in your *RWA*.

_____

_____

_____

Now, diagram your *RWA* using key words from the *RWA* or other words of your choice.

Step 4: Personal/Family Association (PFA)

Write one or more sentences relating the word ***compromise*** to your own personal experience or the personal experience of someone important in your life (e.g., parent, sibling, friend). Make sure the *PFA* expresses your own or chosen others' feelings.

_____

_____

_____

Student Worksheet

_____
Student name

Step 1: Question

_____
Feeling Word

Has anyone ever refused to do something and then finally agreed in order to be able to do what you wanted?

Definition: _____

_____

Step 2: *Design*

Personified Explanation (PE): _____

_____

Step 3: *Real World Association (RWA)*

In what way does the *Design* and PE relate to the "Real World?" Write one or more sentences relating the word _____ to something you've learned in class, a news story, a social event, or anything you feel strongly about. Substitute the symbols in the *Design* for the real people/places/things in your *RWA*.

_____

_____

_____

Now, diagram your *RWA* using key words from the *RWA* or other words of your choice.

Step 4: *Personal/Family Association (PFA)*

Write one or more sentences relating the word _____to your own personal experience or the personal experience of someone important in your life (e.g., parent, sibling, friend). Make sure the *PFA* expresses your own or chosen others' feelings.

_____

_____

_____

Teacher Lesson Sheet

Cope - *to effectively handle a difficult situation*

Step 1: Question
Have you or anyone you know ever had a problem that was hard to deal with? What did you or that person do to help the situation?
Word Introduction: *To **cope** is to effectively deal with a difficult situation.*

Step 2: *Design*

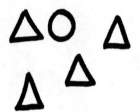

Personified Explanation (PE): *The circle has **coped** with its fear of being in a new environment by becoming friends with one of the triangles.*

Step 3: *Real World Association (RWA)*
In what way does the *Design* and *PE* relate to the "Real World?" Write one or more sentences relating the word ***cope*** to something you've learned in class, a news story, a social event, or anything you feel strongly about. Substitute the symbols in the *Design* for the real people/places/things in your *RWA*.

_____

_____

_____

Now, diagram your *RWA* using key words from the *RWA* or other words of your choice.

Step 4: Personal/Family Association (PFA)
Write one or more sentences relating the word ***cope*** to your own personal experience or the personal experience of someone important in your life (e.g., parent, sibling, friend). Make sure the *PFA* expresses your own or chosen others' feelings.

_____

_____

_____

Student Worksheet

_____
Feeling Word

Step 1: Question
Have you or anyone you know ever had a problem that was hard to deal with? What did you or that person do to help the situation?

Definition: _____
_____

Step 2: *Design*

△O   △
   △
△ △

Personified Explanation (PE): _____
_____

Step 3: *Real World Association (RWA)*
In what way does the *Design* and PE relate to the "Real World?" Write one or more sentences relating the word _____ to something you've learned in class, a news story, a social event, or anything you feel strongly about. Substitute the symbols in the *Design* for the real people/places/things in your *RWA*.

_____

_____

_____

Now, diagram your *RWA* using key words from the *RWA* or other words of your choice.

Step 4: *Personal/Family Association (PFA)*
Write one or more sentences relating the word _____to your own personal experience or the personal experience of someone important in your life (e.g., parent, sibling, friend). Make sure the *PFA* expresses your own or chosen others' feelings.

_____

_____

_____

Teacher Lesson Sheet

Depression - extreme sadness

Step 1: Question
What kind of things make you or people you know feel extremely sad?

Word Introduction: *To be **depressed** is to feel extremely sad.*

Step 2: *Design*

Personified Explanation (PE): *The outside circle feels **depressed** because it's been forced out of the play area and none of the other circles will talk to it or play with it.*

Step 3: *Real World Association (RWA)*
In what way does the *Design* and *PE* relate to the "Real World?" Write one or more sentences relating the word ***depressed*** to something you've learned in class, a news story, a social event, or anything you feel strongly about. Substitute the symbols in the *Design* for the real people/places/things in your *RWA*.

_____

_____

_____

Now, diagram your *RWA* using key words from the *RWA* or other words of your choice.

Step 4: Personal/Family Association (PFA)
Write one or more sentences relating the word ***depressed*** to your own personal experience or the personal experience of someone important in your life (e.g., parent, sibling, friend). Make sure the *PFA* expresses your own or chosen others' feelings.

_____

_____

_____

Student Worksheet

Student name

Step 1: Question

Feeling Word

What kind of things make you or people you know feel extremely sad?

Definition: _____

_____

Step 2: *Design*

Personified Explanation (PE): _____

_____

Step 3: *Real World Association (RWA)*

In what way does the *Design* and PE relate to the "Real World?" Write one or more sentences relating the word _____ to something you've learned in class, a news story, a social event, or anything you feel strongly about. Substitute the symbols in the *Design* for the real people/places/things in your *RWA*.

_____

_____

Now, diagram your *RWA* using key words from the *RWA* or other words of your choice.

Step 4: *Personal/Family Association (PFA)*

Write one or more sentences relating the word _____to your own personal experience or the personal experience of someone important in your life (e.g., parent, sibling, friend). Make sure the *PFA* expresses your own or chosen others' feelings.

_____

_____

_____

Emotional Literacy in the Middle School 115

Teacher Lesson Sheet

Deprivation- *to be without or to not have something that is necessary*

Step 1: Question
What are things that are necessary in a person's life? What can happen if some of these things are taken away?
Word Introduction: *The word **deprivation** means to be without or to remove something that is necessary.*

Step 2: *Design*

Personified Explanation (PE): *The little boxes are **deprived** of their freedom because the larger box refuses to let them out.*

Step 3: *Real World Association (RWA)*
In what way does the *Design* and *PE* relate to the "Real World?" Write one or more sentences relating the word **deprive** to something you've learned in class, a news story, a social event, or anything you feel strongly about. Substitute the symbols in the *Design* for the real people/places/things in your *RWA*.

_____

_____

_____

Now, diagram your *RWA* using key words from the *RWA* or other words of your choice.

Step 4: Personal/Family Association (PFA)
Write one or more sentences relating the word **deprive** to your own personal experience or the personal experience of someone important in your life (e.g., parent, sibling, friend). Make sure the *PFA* expresses your own or chosen others' feelings.

_____

_____

_____

Student Worksheet

Step 1: Question

Feeling Word

What are things that are necessary in a person's life? What can happen if some of these things are taken away?

Definition: _____

_____

Step 2: *Design*

Personified Explanation (PE): _____

_____

Step 3: *Real World Association (RWA)*

In what way does the *Design* and PE relate to the "Real World?" Write one or more sentences relating the word _____ to something you've learned in class, a news story, a social event, or anything you feel strongly about. Substitute the symbols in the *Design* for the real people/places/things in your *RWA*.

_____

_____

Now, diagram your *RWA* using key words from the *RWA* or other words of your choice.

Step 4: *Personal/Family Association (PFA)*

Write one or more sentences relating the word _____to your own personal experience or the personal experience of someone important in your life (e.g., parent, sibling, friend). Make sure the *PFA* expresses your own or chosen others' feelings.

_____

_____

_____

Teacher Lesson Sheet

Despair - feeling hopeless

Step 1: Question
What kind of situations would make you or someone else feel hopeless?

Word Introduction: *The word **despair** means to feel hopeless.*

Step 2: *Design*

*Personified Explanation (PE): The dot feels **despair** because it has been trying to get out of the circle and nothing seems to work.*

Step 3: *Real World Association (RWA)*

In what way does the *Design* and *PE* relate to the "Real World?" Write one or more sentences relating the word **despair** to something you've learned in class, a news story, a social event, or anything you feel strongly about. Substitute the symbols in the *Design* for the real people/places/things in your *RWA*.

_____

_____

_____

Now, diagram your *RWA* using key words from the *RWA* or other words of your choice.

Step 4: *Personal/Family Association (PFA)*

Write one or more sentences relating the word **despair** to your own personal experience or the personal experience of someone important in your life (e.g., parent, sibling, friend). Make sure the *PFA* expresses your own or chosen others' feelings.

_____

_____

_____

Student Worksheet

_____
Student name

Step 1: Question

_____
Feeling Word

What kind of situations would make you or someone else feel hopeless?

Definition: _____
_____

Step 2: *Design*

Personified Explanation (PE): _____
_____

Step 3: *Real World Association (RWA)*
In what way does the *Design* and PE relate to the "Real World?" Write one or more sentences relating the word _____ to something you've learned in class, a news story, a social event, or anything you feel strongly about. Substitute the symbols in the *Design* for the real people/places/things in your *RWA*.

_____

_____

_____

Now, diagram your *RWA* using key words from the *RWA* or other words of your choice.

Step 4: *Personal/Family Association (PFA)*
Write one or more sentences relating the word _____to your own personal experience or the personal experience of someone important in your life (e.g., parent, sibling, friend). Make sure the *PFA* expresses your own or chosen others' feelings.

_____

_____

_____

Teacher Lesson Sheet

Devastated - to feel overwhelmed, shocked, and upset

Step 1: Question
Has something ever happened that really shocked you? What happened?

Word Introduction: *To be **devastated** is to feel overwhelmed, shocked and upset.*

Step 2: *Design*

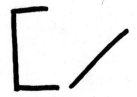

Personified Explanation (PE): *The square is **devastated** because it is falling apart and it doesn't know what to do about it.*

Step 3: *Real World Association (RWA)*
In what way does the *Design* and *PE* relate to the "Real World?" Write one or more sentences relating the word ***devastated*** to something you've learned in class, a news story, a social event, or anything you feel strongly about. Substitute the symbols in the *Design* for the real people/places/things in your *RWA*.

_____

_____

_____

Now, diagram your *RWA* using key words from the *RWA* or other words of your choice.

Step 4: *Personal/Family Association (PFA)*
Write one or more sentences relating the word ***devastated*** to your own personal experience or the personal experience of someone important in your life (e.g., parent, sibling, friend). Make sure the *PFA* expresses your own or chosen others' feelings.

_____

_____

_____

Student Worksheet

_____
Feeling Word

Step 1: Question

Has something ever happened that really shocked you? What happened?

Definition: _____

_____

Step 2: _Design_

Personified Explanation (PE): _____

_____

Step 3: _Real World Association (RWA)_

In what way does the _Design_ and PE relate to the "Real World?" Write one or more
sentences relating the word _____ to something you've learned in class,
a news story, a social event, or anything you feel strongly about. Substitute the
symbols in the _Design_ for the real people/places/things in your _RWA_.

_____

_____

Now, diagram your _RWA_ using key words from the _RWA_ or other words of your choice.

Step 4: _Personal/Family Association (PFA)_

Write one or more sentences relating the word _____ to your own personal
experience or the personal experience of someone important in your life (e.g., parent,
sibling, friend). Make sure the _PFA_ expresses your own or chosen others' feelings.

_____

_____

_____

Teacher Lesson Sheet

Discouraged - to feel frustration and failure

Step 1: Question
Has anyone ever experienced frustration or failure with something they wanted to do?

Word Introduction: *The word **discouraged** means to experience frustration and failure.*

Step 2: *Design*

Personified Explanation (PE): *The circle on the left is **discouraged** because it has continuously tried to jump over the triangle like the other circles and still can't.*

Step 3: *Real World Association (RWA)*

In what way does the *Design* and *PE* relate to the "Real World?" Write one or more sentences relating the word ***discouraged*** to something you've learned in class, a news story, a social event, or anything you feel strongly about. Substitute the symbols in the *Design* for the real people/places/things in your *RWA*.

_____

_____

_____

Now, diagram your *RWA* using key words from the *RWA* or other words of your choice.

Step 4: Personal/Family Association (PFA)
Write one or more sentences relating the word ***discouraged*** to your own personal experience or the personal experience of someone important in your life (e.g., parent, sibling, friend). Make sure the *PFA* expresses your own or chosen others' feelings.

_____

_____

_____

Student Worksheet

Step 1: Question

Feeling Word

Has anyone ever experienced frustration or failure with something they wanted to do?

Definition: _____

_____

Step 2: *Design*

o △ 8

Personified Explanation (PE): _____

_____

Step 3: *Real World Association (RWA)*
In what way does the *Design* and PE relate to the "Real World?" Write one or more sentences relating the word _____ to something you've learned in class, a news story, a social event, or anything you feel strongly about. Substitute the symbols in the *Design* for the real people/places/things in your *RWA*.

_____

_____

_____

Now, diagram your *RWA* using key words from the *RWA* or other words of your choice.

Step 4: *Personal/Family Association (PFA)*
Write one or more sentences relating the word _____to your own personal experience or the personal experience of someone important in your life (e.g., parent, sibling, friend). Make sure the *PFA* expresses your own or chosen others' feelings.

_____

_____

_____

Teacher Lesson Sheet

Empathy - *to relate to and feel deeply for another*

Step 1: Question
Have you ever had deep feelings for someone's illness or misfortune?

Word Introduction: The word **empathy** means to relate to and feel deeply for another.

Step 2: *Design*

Personified Explanation (PE): *The full circle feels* **empathy** *for the sick circle because it can't lead a normal life.*

Step 3: *Real World Association (RWA)*
In what way does the *Design* and *PE* relate to the "Real World?" Write one or more sentences relating the word ***empathy*** to something you've learned in class, a news story, a social event, or anything you feel strongly about. Substitute the symbols in the *Design* for the real people/places/things in your *RWA*.

_____

_____

_____

Now, diagram your *RWA* using key words from the *RWA* or other words of your choice.

Step 4: *Personal/Family Association (PFA)*
Write one or more sentences relating the word ***empathy*** to your own personal experience or the personal experience of someone important in your life (e.g., parent, sibling, friend). Make sure the *PFA* expresses your own or chosen others' feelings.

_____

_____

_____

Student Worksheet

Step 1: Question

_____
Feeling Word

Have you ever had deep feelings for someone's illness or misfortune?

Definition: _____

_____

Step 2: *Design*

O ✿

Personified Explanation (PE): _____

_____

Step 3: *Real World Association (RWA)*

In what way does the *Design* and PE relate to the "Real World?" Write one or more
sentences relating the word _____ to something you've learned in class,
a news story, a social event, or anything you feel strongly about. Substitute the
symbols in the *Design* for the real people/places/things in your *RWA*.

_____

_____

_____

Now, diagram your *RWA* using key words from the *RWA* or other words of your choice.

Step 4: *Personal/Family Association (PFA)*

Write one or more sentences relating the word _____to your own personal
experience or the personal experience of someone important in your life (e.g., parent,
sibling, friend). Make sure the *PFA* expresses your own or chosen others' feelings.

_____

_____

_____

Emotional Literacy in the Middle School 125

Teacher Lesson Sheet

Enraged - *extreme or violent anger*

Step 1: Question
Has anyone ever been or known someone who was extremely angry and didn't know how to handle it?

Word Introduction: *The word **enraged** means to feel extreme violent anger.*

Step 2: *Design*

Personified Explanation (PE): *The Design looks like the word **enraged** because it appears to be angry and out of control.*

Step 3: *Real World Association (RWA)*

In what way does the *Design* and *PE* relate to the "Real World?" Write one or more sentences relating the word ***enraged*** to something you've learned in class, a news story, a social event, or anything you feel strongly about. Substitute the symbols in the *Design* for the real people/places/things in your *RWA*.

_____

_____

_____

Now, diagram your *RWA* using key words from the *RWA* or other words of your choice.

Step 4: Personal/Family Association (PFA)

Write one or more sentences relating the word ***enraged*** to your own personal experience or the personal experience of someone important in your life (e.g., parent, sibling, friend). Make sure the *PFA* expresses your own or chosen others' feelings.

_____

_____

_____

Student Worksheet

Step 1: Question

Feeling Word

Has anyone ever been or known someone who was extremely angry and didn't know how to handle it?

Definition: _____

_____

Step 2: *Design*

Personified Explanation (PE): _____

_____

Step 3: *Real World Association (RWA)*

In what way does the *Design* and PE relate to the "Real World?" Write one or more sentences relating the word _____ to something you've learned in class, a news story, a social event, or anything you feel strongly about. Substitute the symbols in the *Design* for the real people/places/things in your *RWA*.

_____

_____

_____

Now, diagram your *RWA* using key words from the *RWA* or other words of your choice.

Step 4: *Personal/Family Association (PFA)*

Write one or more sentences relating the word _____ to your own personal experience or the personal experience of someone important in your life (e.g., parent, sibling, friend). Make sure the *PFA* expresses your own or chosen others' feelings.

_____

_____

_____

Teacher Lesson Sheet

Enthusiasm - *overjoyed with great interest*

Step 1: Question
What is your greatest interest or desire? What really excites you?

Word Introduction: *To have* **enthusiasm** *is to have great interest in something.*

Step 2: *Design*

Personified Explanation (PE): *The circles are* **enthusiastic** *about the journey to the top because they have been looking forward to the climb for a long time.*

Step 3: *Real World Association (RWA)*

In what way does the *Design* and *PE* relate to the "Real World?" Write one or more sentences relating the word **enthusiastic** to something you've learned in class, a news story, a social event, or anything you feel strongly about. Substitute the symbols in the *Design* for the real people/places/things in your *RWA*.

_____

_____

_____

Now, diagram your *RWA* using key words from the *RWA* or other words of your choice.

Step 4: Personal/Family Association (PFA)

Write one or more sentences relating the word **enthusiastic** to your own personal experience or the personal experience of someone important in your life (e.g., parent, sibling, friend). Make sure the *PFA* expresses your own or chosen others' feelings.

_____

_____

_____

Student Worksheet

Step 1: Question

Feeling Word

What is your greatest interest or desire? What really excites you?

Definition: _____

_____

Step 2: *Design*

Personified Explanation (PE): _____

_____

Step 3: *Real World Association (RWA)*

In what way does the *Design* and PE relate to the "Real World?" Write one or more sentences relating the word _____ to something you've learned in class, a news story, a social event, or anything you feel strongly about. Substitute the symbols in the *Design* for the real people/places/things in your *RWA*.

_____

_____

_____

Now, diagram your *RWA* using key words from the *RWA* or other words of your choice.

Step 4: *Personal/Family Association (PFA)*

Write one or more sentences relating the word _____to your own personal experience or the personal experience of someone important in your life (e.g., parent, sibling, friend). Make sure the *PFA* expresses your own or chosen others' feelings.

_____

_____

_____

Emotional Literacy in the Middle School   129

Teacher Lesson Sheet

Envious - to want what someone else has

Step 1: Question
What makes some people want what others have?

Word Introduction: *To be **envious** is to want what someone else has.*

Step 2: *Design*

*Personified Explanation (PE): The circle on the left is **envious** of the circle on the right because it doesn't have as many dots.*

Step 3: *Real World Association (RWA)*
In what way does the *Design* and *PE* relate to the "Real World?" Write one or more sentences relating the word ***envious*** to something you've learned in class, a news story, a social event, or anything you feel strongly about. Substitute the symbols in the *Design* for the real people/places/things in your *RWA*.

_____

_____

_____

Now, diagram your *RWA* using key words from the *RWA* or other words of your choice.

Step 4: *Personal/Family Association (PFA)*
Write one or more sentences relating the word ***envious*** to your own personal experience or the personal experience of someone important in your life (e.g., parent, sibling, friend). Make sure the *PFA* expresses your own or chosen others' feelings.

_____

_____

_____

Student Worksheet

_____
Student name

_____
Feeling Word

Step 1: Question

What makes some people want what others have?

Definition: _____

_____

Step 2: *Design*

Personified Explanation (PE): _____

_____

Step 3: *Real World Association (RWA)*
In what way does the *Design* and PE relate to the "Real World?" Write one or more sentences relating the word _____ to something you've learned in class, a news story, a social event, or anything you feel strongly about. Substitute the symbols in the *Design* for the real people/places/things in your *RWA*.

_____

_____

_____

Now, diagram your *RWA* using key words from the *RWA* or other words of your choice.

Step 4: *Personal/Family Association (PFA)*
Write one or more sentences relating the word _____to your own personal experience or the personal experience of someone important in your life (e.g., parent, sibling, friend). Make sure the *PFA* expresses your own or chosen others' feelings.

_____

_____

_____

Teacher Lesson Sheet

Exhilaration - *Feeling great and full of energy*

Step 1: Question
How would you feel if your greatest wish came true?

Word Introduction: *To feel **exhilarated** is to feel great and full of energy.*

Step 2: *Design*

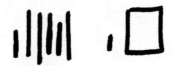

Personified Explanation (PE): *The little line is **exhilarated** over not only keeping up with the bigger lines, but also over its ability to beat all of them to the square.*

Step 3: *Real World Association (RWA)*

In what way does the *Design* and *PE* relate to the "Real World?" Write one or more sentences relating the word ***exhilarated*** to something you've learned in class, a news story, a social event, or anything you feel strongly about. Substitute the symbols in the *Design* for the real people/places/things in your *RWA*.

_____

_____

_____

Now, diagram your *RWA* using key words from the *RWA* or other words of your choice.

Step 4: Personal/Family Association (PFA)

Write one or more sentences relating the word ***exhilarated*** to your own personal experience or the personal experience of someone important in your life (e.g., parent, sibling, friend). Make sure the *PFA* expresses your own or chosen others' feelings.

_____

_____

_____

Student Worksheet

Feeling Word

Step 1: Question

How would you feel if your greatest wish came true?

Definition: _____

_____

Step 2: *Design*

Personified Explanation (PE): _____

_____

Step 3: *Real World Association (RWA)*

In what way does the *Design* and PE relate to the "Real World?" Write one or more sentences relating the word _____ to something you've learned in class, a news story, a social event, or anything you feel strongly about. Substitute the symbols in the *Design* for the real people/places/things in your *RWA*.

_____

_____

_____

Now, diagram your *RWA* using key words from the *RWA* or other words of your choice.

Step 4: *Personal/Family Association (PFA)*

Write one or more sentences relating the word _____ to your own personal experience or the personal experience of someone important in your life (e.g., parent, sibling, friend). Make sure the *PFA* expresses your own or chosen others' feelings.

_____

_____

_____

Teacher Lesson Sheet

Externalize - *expressing your feelings to others*

Step 1: Question
Why is it important to let certain people know how or what you feel?

Word Introduction: *To **externalize** your feelings is to express them to others.*

Step 2: *Design*

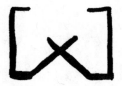

*Personified Explanation (PE): The rectangles are opening up and **externalizing** their feelings to each other because they're very close and want to maintain a good relationship.*

Step 3: *Real World Association (RWA)*

In what way does the *Design* and *PE* relate to the "Real World?" Write one or more sentences relating the word ***externalize*** to something you've learned in class, a news story, a social event, or anything you feel strongly about. Substitute the symbols in the *Design* for the real people/places/things in your *RWA*.

_____

_____

_____

Now, diagram your *RWA* using key words from the *RWA* or other words of your choice.

Step 4: *Personal/Family Association (PFA)*

Write one or more sentences relating the word ***externalize*** to your own personal experience or the personal experience of someone important in your life (e.g., parent, sibling, friend). Make sure the *PFA* expresses your own or chosen others' feelings.

_____

_____

_____

Student Worksheet

Step 1: Question

Feeling Word

Why is it important to let certain people know how or what you feel?

Definition: _____

_____

Step 2: *Design*

Personified Explanation (PE): _____

_____

Step 3: *Real World Association (RWA)*

In what way does the *Design* and PE relate to the "Real World?" Write one or more sentences relating the word _____ to something you've learned in class, a news story, a social event, or anything you feel strongly about. Substitute the symbols in the *Design* for the real people/places/things in your *RWA*.

_____

_____

_____

Now, diagram your *RWA* using key words from the *RWA* or other words of your choice.

Step 4: *Personal/Family Association (PFA)*

Write one or more sentences relating the word _____ to your own personal experience or the personal experience of someone important in your life (e.g., parent, sibling, friend). Make sure the *PFA* expresses your own or chosen others' feelings.

_____

_____

_____

Emotional Literacy in the Middle School   135

Teacher Lesson Sheet

Forlorn - *feeling sad and hopeless*

Step 1: Question
What kind of situation would make someone feel sad and as if he or she were left alone and hopeless?
Word Introduction: *To be **forlorn** is to feel sad and hopeless*

Step 2: *Design*

Personified Explanation (PE): *The lone circle feels **forlorn** because it has been rejected and ignored by the other circles.*

Step 3: *Real World Association (RWA)*

In what way does the *Design* and *PE* relate to the "Real World?" Write one or more sentences relating the word ***forlorn*** to something you've learned in class, a news story, a social event, or anything you feel strongly about. Substitute the symbols in the *Design* for the real people/places/things in your *RWA*.

_____

_____

_____

Now, diagram your *RWA* using key words from the *RWA* or other words of your choice.

Step 4: Personal/Family Association (PFA)

Write one or more sentences relating the word ***forlorn*** to your own personal experience or the personal experience of someone important in your life (e.g., parent, sibling, friend). Make sure the *PFA* expresses your own or chosen others' feelings.

_____

_____

_____

Student Worksheet

Step 1: Question

Feeling Word

What kind of situation would make someone feel sad and as if he or she were left alone and hopeless?

Definition: _____

_____

Step 2: *Design*

Personified Explanation (PE): _____

_____

Step 3: *Real World Association (RWA)*
In what way does the *Design* and PE relate to the "Real World?" Write one or more sentences relating the word _____ to something you've learned in class, a news story, a social event, or anything you feel strongly about. Substitute the symbols in the *Design* for the real people/places/things in your *RWA*.

_____

_____

Now, diagram your *RWA* using key words from the *RWA* or other words of your choice.

Step 4: *Personal/Family Association (PFA)*
Write one or more sentences relating the word _____ to your own personal experience or the personal experience of someone important in your life (e.g., parent, sibling, friend). Make sure the *PFA* expresses your own or chosen others' feelings.

_____

_____

_____

Teacher Lesson Sheet

Frustration - feeling impatient and disappointed

Step 1: Question
How does it feel when you try very hard to do something or fix something and you are not successful?
Word Introduction: *The word **frustration** means to feel impatient and disappointed.*

Step 2: *Design*

Personified Explanation (PE): *The circles are **frustrated** because the line is keeping them from being together*

Step 3: *Real World Association (RWA)*
In what way does the *Design* and *PE* relate to the "Real World?" Write one or more sentences relating the word **frustration** to something you've learned in class, a news story, a social event, or anything you feel strongly about. Substitute the symbols in the *Design* for the real people/places/things in your *RWA*.

_____

_____

_____

Now, diagram your *RWA* using key words from the *RWA* or other words of your choice.

Step 4: Personal/Family Association (PFA)
Write one or more sentences relating the word **frustration** to your own personal experience or the personal experience of someone important in your life (e.g., parent, sibling, friend). Make sure the *PFA* expresses your own or chosen others' feelings.

_____

_____

_____

Student Worksheet

_____
Student name

_____
Feeling Word

Step 1: Question
How does it feel when you try very hard to do something or fix something and you are not successful?

Definition: _____

_____

Step 2: _Design_

o|o

Personified Explanation (PE): _____

_____

Step 3: _Real World Association (RWA)_
In what way does the _Design_ and PE relate to the "Real World?" Write one or more sentences relating the word _____ to something you've learned in class, a news story, a social event, or anything you feel strongly about. Substitute the symbols in the _Design_ for the real people/places/things in your _RWA_.

_____

_____

_____

Now, diagram your _RWA_ using key words from the _RWA_ or other words of your choice.

Step 4: _Personal/Family Association (PFA)_
Write one or more sentences relating the word _____ to your own personal experience or the personal experience of someone important in your life (e.g., parent, sibling, friend). Make sure the _PFA_ expresses your own or chosen others' feelings.

_____

_____

_____

Teacher Lesson Sheet

Greed - to want much more than is necessary

Step 1: Question
Does anyone know someone who constantly wants, wants, and wants and is never satisfied? Give an example.
Word Introduction: *To be **greedy** is to want more than is necessary..*

Step 2: *Design*

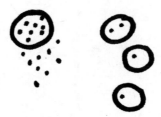

Personified Explanation (PE): *The circle on the left is **greedy** because it already has enough dots but still wants more dots.*

Step 3: *Real World Association (RWA)*

In what way does the *Design* and *PE* relate to the "Real World?" Write one or more sentences relating the word ***greed*** to something you've learned in class, a news story, a social event, or anything you feel strongly about. Substitute the symbols in the *Design* for the real people/places/things in your *RWA*.

_____

_____

_____

Now, diagram your *RWA* using key words from the *RWA* or other words of your choice.

Step 4: Personal/Family Association (PFA)
Write one or more sentences relating the word ***greed*** to your own personal experience or the personal experience of someone important in your life (e.g., parent, sibling, friend). Make sure the *PFA* expresses your own or chosen others' feelings.

_____

_____

_____

Student Worksheet

Step 1: Question

Feeling Word

Does anyone know someone who constantly wants, wants, and wants and is never satisfied? Give an example.

Definition: _____

_____

Step 2: *Design*

Personified Explanation (PE): _____

_____

Step 3: *Real World Association (RWA)*

In what way does the *Design* and PE relate to the "Real World?" Write one or more sentences relating the word _____ to something you've learned in class, a news story, a social event, or anything you feel strongly about. Substitute the symbols in the *Design* for the real people/places/things in your *RWA*.

_____

_____

_____

Now, diagram your *RWA* using key words from the *RWA* or other words of your choice.

Step 4: *Personal/Family Association (PFA)*

Write one or more sentences relating the word _____ to your own personal experience or the personal experience of someone important in your life (e.g., parent, sibling, friend). Make sure the *PFA* expresses your own or chosen others' feelings.

_____

_____

_____

Teacher Lesson Sheet

Guilty - *feeling responsible after doing something wrong*

Step 1: Question
How would you feel if you did something you weren't supposed to do and someone got hurt or something went wrong?
Word Introduction: *To be **guilty** is to feel responsible for doing something wrong.*

Step 2: *Design*

Personified Explanation (PE): *The strong circle who was able to get over the triangle feels **guilty** because it didn't help the other little circles.*

Step 3: *Real World Association (RWA)*

In what way does the *Design* and *PE* relate to the "Real World?" Write one or more sentences relating the word ***guilty*** to something you've learned in class, a news story, a social event, or anything you feel strongly about. Substitute the symbols in the *Design* for the real people/places/things in your *RWA*.

_____

_____

_____

Now, diagram your *RWA* using key words from the *RWA* or other words of your choice.

Step 4: *Personal/Family Association (PFA)*

Write one or more sentences relating the word ***guilty*** to your own personal experience or the personal experience of someone important in your life (e.g., parent, sibling, friend). Make sure the *PFA* expresses your own or chosen others' feelings.

_____

_____

_____

Student Worksheet

Feeling Word

Step 1: Question

How would you feel if you did something you weren't supposed to do and someone got hurt or something went wrong?

Definition: _____

_____

Step 2: *Design*

Personified Explanation (PE): _____

_____

Step 3: *Real World Association (RWA)*

In what way does the *Design* and PE relate to the "Real World?" Write one or more sentences relating the word _____ to something you've learned in class, a news story, a social event, or anything you feel strongly about. Substitute the symbols in the *Design* for the real people/places/things in your *RWA*.

_____

_____

_____

Now, diagram your *RWA* using key words from the *RWA* or other words of your choice.

Step 4: *Personal/Family Association (PFA)*

Write one or more sentences relating the word _____ to your own personal experience or the personal experience of someone important in your life (e.g., parent, sibling, friend). Make sure the *PFA* expresses your own or chosen others' feelings.

_____

_____

_____

Teacher Lesson Sheet

Hostile - *angry and unfriendly*

Step 1: Question
Has anyone ever been around someone who was very unfriendly and angry? Give an example.
Word Introduction: *Someone who is **hostile** is angry and unfriendly.*

Step 2: *Design*

Personified Explanation (PE): *The box is **hostile** towards the inside dot because it won't let it out to play with the other dots.*

Step 3: *Real World Association (RWA)*
In what way does the *Design* and *PE* relate to the "Real World?" Write one or more sentences relating the word ***hostile*** to something you've learned in class, a news story, a social event, or anything you feel strongly about. Substitute the symbols in the *Design* for the real people/places/things in your *RWA*.

_____

_____

_____

Now, diagram your *RWA* using key words from the *RWA* or other words of your choice.

Step 4: Personal/Family Association (PFA)
Write one or more sentences relating the word ***hostile*** to your own personal experience or the personal experience of someone important in your life (e.g., parent, sibling, friend). Make sure the *PFA* expresses your own or chosen others' feelings.

_____

_____

_____

Student Worksheet

_____
Feeling Word

Step 1: Question

Has anyone ever been around someone who was very unfriendly and angry? Give an example.

Definition: _____

_____

Step 2: *Design*

Personified Explanation (PE): _____

_____

Step 3: *Real World Association (RWA)*

In what way does the *Design* and PE relate to the "Real World?" Write one or more sentences relating the word _____ to something you've learned in class, a news story, a social event, or anything you feel strongly about. Substitute the symbols in the *Design* for the real people/places/things in your *RWA*.

_____

_____

Now, diagram your *RWA* using key words from the *RWA* or other words of your choice.

Step 4: *Personal/Family Association (PFA)*

Write one or more sentences relating the word _____to your own personal experience or the personal experience of someone important in your life (e.g., parent, sibling, friend). Make sure the *PFA* expresses your own or chosen others' feelings.

_____

_____

Teacher Lesson Sheet

Humble - not being overly proud

Step 1: Question
How do you feel about people who are always bragging about themselves or what they own?
Word Introduction: *A **humble** person doesn't brag or show off.*

Step 2: *Design*

Personified Explanation (PE): *Even though the top triangle can jump the highest, it is **humble** because it doesn't brag about its ability.*

Step 3: *Real World Association (RWA)*
In what way does the *Design* and *PE* relate to the "Real World?" Write one or more sentences relating the word ***humble*** to something you've learned in class, a news story, a social event, or anything you feel strongly about. Substitute the symbols in the *Design* for the real people/places/things in your *RWA*.

_____

_____

_____

Now, diagram your *RWA* using key words from the *RWA* or other words of your choice.

Step 4: Personal/Family Association (PFA)
Write one or more sentences relating the word ***humble*** to your own personal experience or the personal experience of someone important in your life (e.g., parent, sibling, friend). Make sure the *PFA* expresses your own or chosen others' feelings.

_____

_____

_____

Student Worksheet

_____
Student name

_____
Feeling Word

Step 1: Question

How do you feel about people who are always bragging about themselves or what they own?

Definition: _____

_____

Step 2: *Design*

Personified Explanation (PE): _____

_____

Step 3: *Real World Association (RWA)*

In what way does the *Design* and PE relate to the "Real World?" Write one or more sentences relating the word _____ to something you've learned in class, a news story, a social event, or anything you feel strongly about. Substitute the symbols in the *Design* for the real people/places/things in your *RWA*.

_____

_____

_____

Now, diagram your *RWA* using key words from the *RWA* or other words of your choice.

Step 4: *Personal/Family Association (PFA)*

Write one or more sentences relating the word _____to your own personal experience or the personal experience of someone important in your life (e.g., parent, sibling, friend). Make sure the *PFA* expresses your own or chosen others' feelings.

_____

_____

_____

Teacher Lesson Sheet

Identify - *to relate to a person*

Step 1: Question
Has anyone ever wanted to be like a particular person?

Word Introduction: *To **identify** is to be able to relate to a person.*

Step 2: *Design*

Personified Explanation (PE): *The two jagged lines **identify** with each other because they have similar characteristics.*

Step 3: *Real World Association (RWA)*

In what way does the *Design* and *PE* relate to the "Real World?" Write one or more sentences relating the word ***identifies*** to something you've learned in class, a news story, a social event, or anything you feel strongly about. Substitute the symbols in the *Design* for the real people/places/things in your *RWA*.

_____

_____

_____

Now, diagram your *RWA* using key words from the *RWA* or other words of your choice.

Step 4: Personal/Family Association (PFA)

Write one or more sentences relating the word ***identifies*** to your own personal experience or the personal experience of someone important in your life (e.g., parent, sibling, friend). Make sure the *PFA* expresses your own or chosen others' feelings.

_____

_____

_____

Student Worksheet

_____
Student name

Step 1: Question

_____
Feeling Word

Has anyone ever wanted to be like a particular person?

Definition: _____
_____

Step 2: *Design*

Personified Explanation (PE): _____
_____

Step 3: *Real World Association (RWA)*

In what way does the *Design* and PE relate to the "Real World?" Write one or more sentences relating the word _____ to something you've learned in class, a news story, a social event, or anything you feel strongly about. Substitute the symbols in the *Design* for the real people/places/things in your *RWA*.

_____

_____

Now, diagram your *RWA* using key words from the *RWA* or other words of your choice.

Step 4: *Personal/Family Association (PFA)*

Write one or more sentences relating the word _____ to your own personal experience or the personal experience of someone important in your life (e.g., parent, sibling, friend). Make sure the *PFA* expresses your own or chosen others' feelings.

_____

_____

_____

Teacher Lesson Sheet

Impulsive - *something done suddenly without thinking*

Step 1: Question
Have you ever done something fast or suddenly without thinking about the consequences?
Word Introduction: *The word **impulsive** means to do something fast or suddenly without thinking about it.*

Step 2: *Design*

Personified Explanation (PE): *The outside circle is **impulsive** because it left the protection of the square in spite of being told that the triangles are dangerous.*

Step 3: *Real World Association (RWA)*

In what way does the *Design* and *PE* relate to the "Real World?" Write one or more sentences relating the word ***impulsive*** to something you've learned in class, a news story, a social event, or anything you feel strongly about. Substitute the symbols in the *Design* for the real people/places/things in your *RWA*.

_____

_____

_____

Now, diagram your *RWA* using key words from the *RWA* or other words of your choice.

Step 4: *Personal/Family Association (PFA)*

Write one or more sentences relating the word ***impulsive*** to your own personal experience or the personal experience of someone important in your life (e.g., parent, sibling, friend). Make sure the *PFA* expresses your own or chosen others' feelings.

_____

_____

_____

Student Worksheet

Step 1: Question

Feeling Word

Have you ever done something fast or suddenly without thinking about the consequences?

Definition: _____

_____

Step 2: *Design*

Personified Explanation (PE): _____

_____

Step 3: *Real World Association (RWA)*
In what way does the *Design* and PE relate to the "Real World?" Write one or more sentences relating the word _____ to something you've learned in class, a news story, a social event, or anything you feel strongly about. Substitute the symbols in the *Design* for the real people/places/things in your *RWA*.

_____

_____

_____

Now, diagram your *RWA* using key words from the *RWA* or other words of your choice.

Step 4: *Personal/Family Association (PFA)*
Write one or more sentences relating the word _____to your own personal experience or the personal experience of someone important in your life (e.g., parent, sibling, friend). Make sure the *PFA* expresses your own or chosen others' feelings.

_____

_____

_____

Emotional Literacy in the Middle School 151

Teacher Lesson Sheet

Indivisible - can't be separated

Step 1: Question
What is the one thing you would refuse to be separated from in your life?

Word Introduction: *Things that are **indivisible** can't be separated.*

Step 2: *Design*

Personified Explanation (PE): *The two vertical lines have become **indivisible** from each other because of the horizontal line.*

Step 3: *Real World Association (RWA)*

In what way does the *Design* and *PE* relate to the "Real World?" Write one or more sentences relating the word ***indivisible*** to something you've learned in class, a news story, a social event, or anything you feel strongly about. Substitute the symbols in the *Design* for the real people/places/things in your *RWA*.

_____

_____

_____

Now, diagram your *RWA* using key words from the *RWA* or other words of your choice.

Step 4: *Personal/Family Association (PFA)*

Write one or more sentences relating the word ***indivisible*** to your own personal experience or the personal experience of someone important in your life (e.g., parent, sibling, friend). Make sure the *PFA* expresses your own or chosen others' feelings.

_____

_____

_____

Student Worksheet

_____
Feeling Word

Step 1: Question

What is the one thing you would refuse to be separated from in your life?

Definition: _____

_____

Step 2: _Design_

**Personified Explanation (PE):** _____

_____

Step 3: _Real World Association (RWA)_

In what way does the _Design_ and PE relate to the "Real World?" Write one or more sentences relating the word _____ to something you've learned in class, a news story, a social event, or anything you feel strongly about. Substitute the symbols in the _Design_ for the real people/places/things in your _RWA_.

_____

_____

_____

Now, diagram your _RWA_ using key words from the _RWA_ or other words of your choice.

Step 4: _Personal/Family Association (PFA)_

Write one or more sentences relating the word _____to your own personal experience or the personal experience of someone important in your life (e.g., parent, sibling, friend). Make sure the _PFA_ expresses your own or chosen others' feelings.

_____

_____

_____

Emotional Literacy in the Middle School   153

Teacher Lesson Sheet

Inhibition - *not feeling free to express yourself*

Step 1: Question
What are some of the reasons why people don't fully express their thoughts, feelings, and desires?
Word Introduction: *To be* **inhibited** *is to not be able to freely express yourself.*

Step 2: *Design*

Personified Explanation (PE): The square on the left is **inhibited** *because the big squares told it that little squares should be heard and not seen.*

Step 3: *Real World Association (RWA)*

In what way does the *Design* and *PE* relate to the "Real World?" Write one or more sentences relating the word **inhibition** to something you've learned in class, a news story, a social event, or anything you feel strongly about. Substitute the symbols in the *Design* for the real people/places/things in your *RWA*.

_____

_____

_____

Now, diagram your *RWA* using key words from the *RWA* or other words of your choice.

Step 4: Personal/Family Association (PFA)
Write one or more sentences relating the word **inhibition** to your own personal experience or the personal experience of someone important in your life (e.g., parent, sibling, friend). Make sure the *PFA* expresses your own or chosen others' feelings.

_____

_____

_____

Student Worksheet

Feeling Word

Step 1: Question

What are some of the reasons why people don't fully express their thoughts, feelings, and desires?

Definition: _____

_____

Step 2: *Design*

Personified Explanation (PE): _____

_____

Step 3: *Real World Association (RWA)*

In what way does the *Design* and PE relate to the "Real World?" Write one or more sentences relating the word _____ to something you've learned in class, a news story, a social event, or anything you feel strongly about. Substitute the symbols in the *Design* for the real people/places/things in your *RWA*.

_____

_____

Now, diagram your *RWA* using key words from the *RWA* or other words of your choice.

Step 4: *Personal/Family Association (PFA)*

Write one or more sentences relating the word _____ to your own personal experience or the personal experience of someone important in your life (e.g., parent, sibling, friend). Make sure the *PFA* expresses your own or chosen others' feelings.

_____

_____

_____

Teacher Lesson Sheet

Insecure - lacking self-confidence

Step 1: Question
What are some of things you would like to do but don't feel confident enough to attempt doing it?
Word Introduction: *To be **insecure** is to lack self-confidence.*

Step 2: *Design*

Personified Explanation (PE): *Even though the lone cross is capable of playing the game, it won't, because it is **insecure**.*

Step 3: *Real World Association (RWA)*

In what way does the *Design* and *PE* relate to the "Real World?" Write one or more sentences relating the word ***insecure*** to something you've learned in class, a news story, a social event, or anything you feel strongly about. Substitute the symbols in the *Design* for the real people/places/things in your *RWA*.

_____

_____

_____

Now, diagram your *RWA* using key words from the *RWA* or other words of your choice.

Step 4: Personal/Family Association (PFA)

Write one or more sentences relating the word ***insecure*** to your own personal experience or the personal experience of someone important in your life (e.g., parent, sibling, friend). Make sure the *PFA* expresses your own or chosen others' feelings.

_____

_____

_____

Student Worksheet

_____
Student name

_____
Feeling Word

Step 1: Question
What are some of things you would like to do but don't feel confident enough to attempt doing it?

Definition: _____

_____

Step 2: *Design*

X X X
X X X X
X X X   X
X X X

Personified Explanation (PE): _____

_____

Step 3: *Real World Association (RWA)*
In what way does the *Design* and PE relate to the "Real World?" Write one or more sentences relating the word _____ to something you've learned in class, a news story, a social event, or anything you feel strongly about. Substitute the symbols in the *Design* for the real people/places/things in your *RWA*.

_____

_____

_____

Now, diagram your *RWA* using key words from the *RWA* or other words of your choice.

Step 4: *Personal/Family Association (PFA)*
Write one or more sentences relating the word _____ to your own personal experience or the personal experience of someone important in your life (e.g., parent, sibling, friend). Make sure the *PFA* expresses your own or chosen others' feelings.

_____

_____

_____

Teacher Lesson Sheet

Internalize - to hold feelings inside

Step 1: Question

What can happen when you hold certain feelings inside that should really be expressed.

Word Introduction: *To **internalize** is to hold thoughts and feelings inside.*

Step 2: *Design*

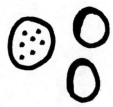

Personified Explanation (PE): *The circle on the left is **internalizing** its sad feelings because it fears what the other circles will think of it.*

Step 3: *Real World Association (RWA)*

In what way does the *Design* and *PE* relate to the "Real World?" Write one or more sentences relating the word ***internalize*** to something you've learned in class, a news story, a social event, or anything you feel strongly about. Substitute the symbols in the *Design* for the real people/places/things in your *RWA*.

_____

_____

_____

Now, diagram your *RWA* using key words from the *RWA* or other words of your choice.

Step 4: *Personal/Family Association (PFA)*

Write one or more sentences relating the word ***internalize*** to your own personal experience or the personal experience of someone important in your life (e.g., parent, sibling, friend). Make sure the *PFA* expresses your own or chosen others' feelings.

_____

_____

_____

Student Worksheet

Step 1: Question

Feeling Word

What can happen when you hold certain feelings inside that should really be expressed.

Definition: _____

_____

Step 2: *Design*

Personified Explanation (PE): _____

_____

Step 3: *Real World Association (RWA)*

In what way does the *Design* and PE relate to the "Real World?" Write one or more sentences relating the word _____ to something you've learned in class, a news story, a social event, or anything you feel strongly about. Substitute the symbols in the *Design* for the real people/places/things in your *RWA*.

_____

_____

_____

Now, diagram your *RWA* using key words from the *RWA* or other words of your choice.

Step 4: *Personal/Family Association (PFA)*

Write one or more sentences relating the word _____ to your own personal experience or the personal experience of someone important in your life (e.g., parent, sibling, friend). Make sure the *PFA* expresses your own or chosen others' feelings.

_____

_____

_____

Teacher Lesson Sheet

Intimate - a close relationship

Step 1: Question
How important are strong friendships? What are some characteristics of a good relationship?
Word Introduction: *To be **intimate** is to have a very close relationship.*

Step 2: *Design*

Personified Explanation (PE): *The circle and the triangle have become **intimate** because they truly trust each other and enjoy each other's company.*

Step 3: *Real World Association (RWA)*

In what way does the *Design* and *PE* relate to the "Real World?" Write one or more sentences relating the word ***intimate*** to something you've learned in class, a news story, a social event, or anything you feel strongly about. Substitute the symbols in the *Design* for the real people/places/things in your *RWA*.

_____

_____

_____

Now, diagram your *RWA* using key words from the *RWA* or other words of your choice.

Step 4: Personal/Family Association (PFA)

Write one or more sentences relating the word ***intimate*** to your own personal experience or the personal experience of someone important in your life (e.g., parent, sibling, friend). Make sure the *PFA* expresses your own or chosen others' feelings.

_____

_____

_____

Student Worksheet

Feeling Word

Step 1: Question
How important are strong friendships? What are some characteristics of a good relationship?

Definition: _____

_____

Step 2: *Design*

Personified Explanation (PE): _____

_____

Step 3: *Real World Association (RWA)*
In what way does the *Design* and PE relate to the "Real World?" Write one or more sentences relating the word _____ to something you've learned in class, a news story, a social event, or anything you feel strongly about. Substitute the symbols in the *Design* for the real people/places/things in your *RWA*.

_____

_____

_____

Now, diagram your *RWA* using key words from the *RWA* or other words of your choice.

Step 4: *Personal/Family Association (PFA)*
Write one or more sentences relating the word _____ to your own personal experience or the personal experience of someone important in your life (e.g., parent, sibling, friend). Make sure the *PFA* expresses your own or chosen others' feelings.

_____

_____

_____

Teacher Lesson Sheet

Irrational - *unreasonable or senseless behavior*

Step 1: Question
Has anyone ever met someone who acted unreasonable, weird and strange? What did he or she do?
Word Introduction: *Irrational people act unreasonably or senseless.*

Step 2: *Design*

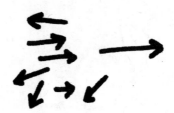

Personified Explanation (PE): *The arrow on the right is clearly **irrational** because it thinks the other arrows will follow it and do whatever it does*

Step 3: *Real World Association (RWA)*
In what way does the *Design* and *PE* relate to the "Real World?" Write one or more sentences relating the word ***irrational*** to something you've learned in class, a news story, a social event, or anything you feel strongly about. Substitute the symbols in the *Design* for the real people/places/things in your *RWA*.

_____

_____

_____

Now, diagram your *RWA* using key words from the *RWA* or other words of your choice.

Step 4: *Personal/Family Association (PFA)*
Write one or more sentences relating the word ***irrational*** to your own personal experience or the personal experience of someone important in your life (e.g., parent, sibling, friend). Make sure the *PFA* expresses your own or chosen others' feelings.

_____

_____

_____

Student Worksheet

Feeling Word

Step 1: Question
Has anyone ever met someone who acted unreasonable, weird and strange? What did he or she do?

Definition: _____

_____

Step 2: *Design*

Personified Explanation (PE): _____

_____

Step 3: *Real World Association (RWA)*
In what way does the *Design* and PE relate to the "Real World?" Write one or more sentences relating the word _____ to something you've learned in class, a news story, a social event, or anything you feel strongly about. Substitute the symbols in the *Design* for the real people/places/things in your *RWA*.

_____

_____

_____

Now, diagram your *RWA* using key words from the *RWA* or other words of your choice.

Step 4: *Personal/Family Association (PFA)*
Write one or more sentences relating the word _____ to your own personal experience or the personal experience of someone important in your life (e.g., parent, sibling, friend). Make sure the *PFA* expresses your own or chosen others' feelings.

_____

_____

_____

Teacher Lesson Sheet

Jubilant - Jumping for joy

Step 1: Question
What has been the single most enjoyable moment in your life?

Word Introduction: *To be **jubilant** is to be jumping for joy*

Step 2: *Design*

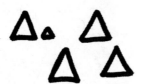

Personified Explanation (PE): *The small triangle feels **jubilant** because after many refusals, the other triangles have accepted it as a member of the group.*

Step 3: *Real World Association (RWA)*

In what way does the *Design* and *PE* relate to the "Real World?" Write one or more sentences relating the word ***jubilant*** to something you've learned in class, a news story, a social event, or anything you feel strongly about. Substitute the symbols in the *Design* for the real people/places/things in your *RWA*.

_____

_____

_____

Now, diagram your *RWA* using key words from the *RWA* or other words of your choice.

Step 4: *Personal/Family Association (PFA)*

Write one or more sentences relating the word ***jubilant*** to your own personal experience or the personal experience of someone important in your life (e.g., parent, sibling, friend). Make sure the *PFA* expresses your own or chosen others' feelings.

_____

_____

_____

Student Worksheet

Step 1: Question

Feeling Word

What has been the single most enjoyable moment in your life?

Definition: _____

_____

Step 2: *Design*

Personified Explanation (PE): _____

_____

Step 3: *Real World Association (RWA)*
In what way does the *Design* and PE relate to the "Real World?" Write one or more sentences relating the word _____ to something you've learned in class, a news story, a social event, or anything you feel strongly about. Substitute the symbols in the *Design* for the real people/places/things in your *RWA*.

_____

_____

Now, diagram your *RWA* using key words from the *RWA* or other words of your choice.

Step 4: *Personal/Family Association (PFA)*
Write one or more sentences relating the word _____to your own personal experience or the personal experience of someone important in your life (e.g., parent, sibling, friend). Make sure the *PFA* expresses your own or chosen others' feelings.

_____

_____

Teacher Lesson Sheet

Loathe - to "really" hate

Step 1: Question
Has anyone ever "really" hated someone for the way he or she acted?

Word Introduction: *The word **loathe** means to "really" hate something or someone.*

Step 2: *Design*

Personified Explanation (PE): *The little line **loathes** the big lines because the big lines continue to make fun of it and are mean.*

Step 3: *Real World Association (RWA)*
In what way does the *Design* and *PE* relate to the "Real World?" Write one or more sentences relating the word ***loathe*** to something you've learned in class, a news story, a social event, or anything you feel strongly about. Substitute the symbols in the *Design* for the real people/places/things in your *RWA*.

_____

_____

_____

Now, diagram your *RWA* using key words from the *RWA* or other words of your choice.

Step 4: Personal/Family Association (PFA)
Write one or more sentences relating the word ***loathe*** to your own personal experience or the personal experience of someone important in your life (e.g., parent, sibling, friend). Make sure the *PFA* expresses your own or chosen others' feelings.

_____

_____

_____

Student Worksheet

Step 1: Question

Feeling Word

Has anyone ever "really" hated someone for the way he or she acted?

Definition: _____

_____

Step 2: *Design*

| |ı |ıı| ·

Personified Explanation (PE): _____

_____

Step 3: *Real World Association (RWA)*

In what way does the *Design* and PE relate to the "Real World?" Write one or more sentences relating the word _____ to something you've learned in class, a news story, a social event, or anything you feel strongly about. Substitute the symbols in the *Design* for the real people/places/things in your *RWA*.

_____

_____

_____

Now, diagram your *RWA* using key words from the *RWA* or other words of your choice.

Step 4: *Personal/Family Association (PFA)*

Write one or more sentences relating the word _____ to your own personal experience or the personal experience of someone important in your life (e.g., parent, sibling, friend). Make sure the *PFA* expresses your own or chosen others' feelings.

_____

_____

_____

Teacher Lesson Sheet

Loyalty - *faithful or devoted*

Step 1: Question
What does being faithful or devoted mean to you? In what ways do we show how faithful we are (e.g. friends, family, etc.)?
Word Introduction: *To be **loyal** is to be faithful or devoted.*

Step 2: *Design*

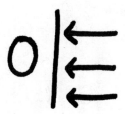

Personified Explanation (PE): *The line is showing its **loyalty** to the circle because it placed itself in the way of the deadly arrows.*

Step 3: *Real World Association (RWA)*
In what way does the *Design* and *PE* relate to the "Real World?" Write one or more sentences relating the word ***loyalty*** to something you've learned in class, a news story, a social event, or anything you feel strongly about. Substitute the symbols in the *Design* for the real people/places/things in your *RWA*.

_____

_____

_____

Now, diagram your *RWA* using key words from the *RWA* or other words of your choice.

Step 4: Personal/Family Association (PFA)
Write one or more sentences relating the word ***loyalty*** to your own personal experience or the personal experience of someone important in your life (e.g., parent, sibling, friend). Make sure the *PFA* expresses your own or chosen others' feelings.

_____

_____

_____

Student Worksheet

Step 1: Question

Feeling Word

What does being faithful or devoted mean to you? In what ways do we show how faithful we are (e.g. friends, family, etc.)?

Definition: _____

_____

Step 2: *Design*

Personified Explanation (PE): _____

_____

Step 3: *Real World Association (RWA)*
In what way does the *Design* and PE relate to the "Real World?" Write one or more sentences relating the word _____ to something you've learned in class, a news story, a social event, or anything you feel strongly about. Substitute the symbols in the *Design* for the real people/places/things in your *RWA.*

_____

_____

Now, diagram your *RWA* using key words from the *RWA* or other words of your choice.

Step 4: *Personal/Family Association (PFA)*
Write one or more sentences relating the word _____ to your own personal experience or the personal experience of someone important in your life (e.g., parent, sibling, friend). Make sure the *PFA* expresses your own or chosen others' feelings.

_____

_____

_____

Teacher Lesson Sheet

Masochistic - *tending to invite or enjoy misery*

Step 1: Question
What kind of person would tend to invite or enjoy misery?

Word Introduction: *To be **masochistic** is to tend to invite or enjoy misery.*

Step 2: *Design*

Personified Explanation (PE): *The circle is **masochistic** because it enjoys being hurt by all of the arrows.*

Step 3: *Real World Association (RWA)*

In what way does the *Design* and *PE* relate to the "Real World?" Write one or more sentences relating the word **masochistic** to something you've learned in class, a news story, a social event, or anything you feel strongly about. Substitute the symbols in the *Design* for the real people/places/things in your *RWA*.

_____

_____

_____

Now, diagram your *RWA* using key words from the *RWA* or other words of your choice.

Step 4: *Personal/Family Association (PFA)*

Write one or more sentences relating the word **masochistic** to your own personal experience or the personal experience of someone important in your life (e.g., parent, sibling, friend). Make sure the *PFA* expresses your own or chosen others' feelings.

_____

_____

_____

Student Worksheet

Step 1: Question

Feeling Word

What kind of person would tend to invite or enjoy misery?

Definition: _____

_____

Step 2: *Design*

Personified Explanation (PE): _____

_____

Step 3: *Real World Association (RWA)*

In what way does the *Design* and PE relate to the "Real World?" Write one or more sentences relating the word _____ to something you've learned in class, a news story, a social event, or anything you feel strongly about. Substitute the symbols in the *Design* for the real people/places/things in your *RWA*.

_____

_____

_____

Now, diagram your *RWA* using key words from the *RWA* or other words of your choice.

Step 4: *Personal/Family Association (PFA)*

Write one or more sentences relating the word _____ to your own personal experience or the personal experience of someone important in your life (e.g., parent, sibling, friend). Make sure the *PFA* expresses your own or chosen others' feelings.

_____

_____

_____

Teacher Lesson Sheet

Motivation - *wanting to accomplish something*

Step 1: Question
What do successful people have in common?

Word Introduction: *To be **motivated** is to really want to accomplish something.*

Step 2: *Design*

Personified Explanation (PE): *This Design looks like the word **motivation** because the arrows won't give up searching for what they want and will continue to go in any direction in order to achieve their goals.*

Step 3: *Real World Association (RWA)*

In what way does the *Design* and *PE* relate to the "Real World?" Write one or more sentences relating the word ***motivation*** to something you've learned in class, a news story, a social event, or anything you feel strongly about. Substitute the symbols in the *Design* for the real people/places/things in your *RWA*.

_____

_____

_____

Now, diagram your *RWA* using key words from the *RWA* or other words of your choice.

Step 4: Personal/Family Association (PFA)

Write one or more sentences relating the word ***motivation*** to your own personal experience or the personal experience of someone important in your life (e.g., parent, sibling, friend). Make sure the *PFA* expresses your own or chosen others' feelings.

_____

_____

_____

Student Worksheet

Step 1: Question

Feeling Word

What do successful people have in common?

Definition: _____

_____

Step 2: *Design*

Personified Explanation (PE): _____

_____

Step 3: *Real World Association (RWA)*

In what way does the *Design* and PE relate to the "Real World?" Write one or more
sentences relating the word _____ to something you've learned in class,
a news story, a social event, or anything you feel strongly about. Substitute the
symbols in the *Design* for the real people/places/things in your *RWA*.

_____

_____

_____

Now, diagram your *RWA* using key words from the *RWA* or other words of your choice.

Step 4: *Personal/Family Association (PFA)*

Write one or more sentences relating the word _____ to your own personal
experience or the personal experience of someone important in your life (e.g., parent,
sibling, friend). Make sure the *PFA* expresses your own or chosen others' feelings.

_____

_____

_____

Teacher Lesson Sheet

Obsession - *a disturbing and uncontrollable thought or feeling*

Step 1: Question
Has anyone ever had a feeling or idea that could not be controlled - such as worrying about something all the time or checking the answers on a quiz over and over?
Word Introduction: The word **obsession** means to have disturbing uncontrollable thoughts.

Step 2: *Design*

Personified Explanation (PE): The line is **obsessed** because it is going around and around and feels it is unable to stop.

Step 3: *Real World Association (RWA)*

In what way does the *Design* and *PE* relate to the "Real World?" Write one or more sentences relating the word **obsessed** to something you've learned in class, a news story, a social event, or anything you feel strongly about. Substitute the symbols in the *Design* for the real people/places/things in your *RWA*.

_____

_____

_____

Now, diagram your *RWA* using key words from the *RWA* or other words of your choice.

Step 4: Personal/Family Association (PFA)
Write one or more sentences relating the word **obsessed** to your own personal experience or the personal experience of someone important in your life (e.g., parent, sibling, friend). Make sure the *PFA* expresses your own or chosen others' feelings.

_____

_____

_____

Student Worksheet

Step 1: Question

Feeling Word

Has anyone ever had a feeling or idea that could not be controlled - such as worrying about something all the time or checking the answers on a quiz over and over?

Definition: _____

_____

Step 2: *Design*

Personified Explanation (PE): _____

_____

Step 3: *Real World Association (RWA)*
In what way does the *Design* and PE relate to the "Real World?" Write one or more sentences relating the word _____ to something you've learned in class, a news story, a social event, or anything you feel strongly about. Substitute the symbols in the *Design* for the real people/places/things in your *RWA*.

_____

_____

Now, diagram your *RWA* using key words from the *RWA* or other words of your choice.

Step 4: *Personal/Family Association (PFA)*
Write one or more sentences relating the word _____to your own personal experience or the personal experience of someone important in your life (e.g., parent, sibling, friend). Make sure the *PFA* expresses your own or chosen others' feelings.

_____

_____

Teacher Lesson Sheet

Optimism - *positive expectations*

Step 1: Question
Have you or has anyone you know ever felt really positive about accomplishing something?
Word Introduction: *The word **optimism** means to have positive expectations.*

Step 2: *Design*

Personified Explanation (PE): *Unlike the circles on the bottom, the circles who were **optimistic** were able to accomplish their goals by getting to the top of the rectangle.*

Step 3: *Real World Association (RWA)*

In what way does the *Design* and *PE* relate to the "Real World?" Write one or more sentences relating the word ***optimistic*** to something you've learned in class, a news story, a social event, or anything you feel strongly about. Substitute the symbols in the *Design* for the real people/places/things in your *RWA*.

_____

_____

_____

Now, diagram your *RWA* using key words from the *RWA* or other words of your choice.

Step 4: *Personal/Family Association (PFA)*

Write one or more sentences relating the word ***optimistic*** to your own personal experience or the personal experience of someone important in your life (e.g., parent, sibling, friend). Make sure the *PFA* expresses your own or chosen others' feelings.

_____

_____

_____

Student Worksheet

Step 1: Question

Feeling Word

Have you or has anyone you know ever felt really positive about accomplishing something?

Definition: _____

_____

Step 2: *Design*

Personified Explanation (PE): _____

_____

Step 3: *Real World Association (RWA)*

In what way does the *Design* and PE relate to the "Real World?" Write one or more sentences relating the word _____ to something you've learned in class, a news story, a social event, or anything you feel strongly about. Substitute the symbols in the *Design* for the real people/places/things in your *RWA*.

_____

_____

_____

Now, diagram your *RWA* using key words from the *RWA* or other words of your choice.

Step 4: *Personal/Family Association (PFA)*

Write one or more sentences relating the word _____to your own personal experience or the personal experience of someone important in your life (e.g., parent, sibling, friend). Make sure the *PFA* expresses your own or chosen others' feelings.

_____

_____

_____

Emotional Literacy in the Middle School   177

Teacher Lesson Sheet

Patience - ability to wait and be calm

Step 1: Question
Why is it important not to rush through difficult tasks and to be calm when trying to accomplish something difficult?
Word Introduction: *To be **patient** is to have the ability to wait and be calm.*

Step 2: *Design*

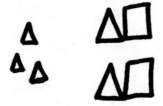

Personified Explanation (PE): *The little triangles have learned the importance of **patience** because they are willing to wait until they grow up before getting their own square.*

Step 3: *Real World Association (RWA)*

In what way does the *Design* and *PE* relate to the "Real World?" Write one or more sentences relating the word ***patience*** to something you've learned in class, a news story, a social event, or anything you feel strongly about. Substitute the symbols in the *Design* for the real people/places/things in your *RWA*.

_____

_____

_____

Now, diagram your *RWA* using key words from the *RWA* or other words of your choice.

Step 4: Personal/Family Association (PFA)

Write one or more sentences relating the word ***patience*** to your own personal experience or the personal experience of someone important in your life (e.g., parent, sibling, friend). Make sure the *PFA* expresses your own or chosen others' feelings.

_____

_____

_____

Student Worksheet

Step 1: Question

Feeling Word

Why is it important not to rush through difficult tasks and to be calm when trying to accomplish something difficult?

Definition: _____

_____

Step 2: *Design*

Personified Explanation (PE): _____

_____

Step 3: *Real World Association (RWA)*

In what way does the *Design* and PE relate to the "Real World?" Write one or more sentences relating the word _____ to something you've learned in class, a news story, a social event, or anything you feel strongly about. Substitute the symbols in the *Design* for the real people/places/things in your *RWA.*

_____

_____

_____

Now, diagram your *RWA* using key words from the *RWA* or other words of your choice.

Step 4: *Personal/Family Association (PFA)*

Write one or more sentences relating the word _____to your own personal experience or the personal experience of someone important in your life (e.g., parent, sibling, friend). Make sure the *PFA* expresses your own or chosen others' feelings.

_____

_____

_____

Teacher Lesson Sheet

Pessimism - to have negative expectations

Step 1: Question
What can and probably will happen when you feel or think you will fail at something?
Give an example.
Word Introduction: *To be **pessimistic** is to have negative expectations.*

Step 2: *Design*

Personified Explanation (PE): *The lone circle will probably never get on top of the rectangle (like the other circles) because it is **pessimistic**.*

Step 3: *Real World Association (RWA)*

In what way does the *Design* and *PE* relate to the "Real World?" Write one or more sentences relating the word ***pessimistic*** to something you've learned in class, a news story, a social event, or anything you feel strongly about. Substitute the symbols in the *Design* for the real people/places/things in your *RWA*.

_____

_____

_____

Now, diagram your *RWA* using key words from the *RWA* or other words of your choice.

Step 4: *Personal/Family Association (PFA)*
Write one or more sentences relating the word ***pessimistic*** to your own personal experience or the personal experience of someone important in your life (e.g., parent, sibling, friend). Make sure the *PFA* expresses your own or chosen others' feelings.

_____

_____

_____

Student Worksheet

_____
Feeling Word

Step 1: Question

What can and probably will happen when you feel or think you will fail at something? Give an example.

Definition: _____

_____

Step 2: _Design_

**Personified Explanation (PE):** _____

_____

Step 3: _Real World Association (RWA)_

In what way does the _Design_ and PE relate to the "Real World?" Write one or more sentences relating the word _____ to something you've learned in class, a news story, a social event, or anything you feel strongly about. Substitute the symbols in the _Design_ for the real people/places/things in your _RWA_.

_____

_____

_____

Now, diagram your _RWA_ using key words from the _RWA_ or other words of your choice.

Step 4: _Personal/Family Association (PFA)_

Write one or more sentences relating the word _____to your own personal experience or the personal experience of someone important in your life (e.g., parent, sibling, friend). Make sure the _PFA_ expresses your own or chosen others' feelings.

_____

_____

_____

Teacher Lesson Sheet

Prejudice - *closed or narrow minded, dislike without reason*

Step 1: Question

What kinds of serious problems often exist because of close-minded people who think they are superior, smarter, etc. than others?

Word Introduction: *To be* **prejudice** *is to be closed or narrow minded and dislike someone for no reason.*

Step 2: *Design*

Personified Explanation (PE): The circles are **prejudice** *toward the triangles because they think they are superior.*

Step 3: *Real World Association (RWA)*

In what way does the *Design* and *PE* relate to the "Real World?" Write one or more sentences relating the word **prejudice** to something you've learned in class, a news story, a social event, or anything you feel strongly about. Substitute the symbols in the *Design* for the real people/places/things in your *RWA*.

_____

_____

_____

Now, diagram your *RWA* using key words from the *RWA* or other words of your choice.

Step 4: *Personal/Family Association (PFA)*

Write one or more sentences relating the word **prejudice** to your own personal experience or the personal experience of someone important in your life (e.g., parent, sibling, friend). Make sure the *PFA* expresses your own or chosen others' feelings.

_____

_____

_____

Student Worksheet

Feeling Word

Step 1: Question

What kinds of serious problems often exist because of close-minded people who think they are superior, smarter, etc. than others?

Definition: _____

_____

Step 2: *Design*

Personified Explanation (PE): _____

_____

Step 3: *Real World Association (RWA)*

In what way does the *Design* and PE relate to the "Real World?" Write one or more sentences relating the word _____ to something you've learned in class, a news story, a social event, or anything you feel strongly about. Substitute the symbols in the *Design* for the real people/places/things in your *RWA*.

_____

_____

_____

Now, diagram your *RWA* using key words from the *RWA* or other words of your choice.

Step 4: *Personal/Family Association (PFA)*

Write one or more sentences relating the word _____ to your own personal experience or the personal experience of someone important in your life (e.g., parent, sibling, friend). Make sure the *PFA* expresses your own or chosen others' feelings.

_____

_____

_____

Teacher Lesson Sheet

Pride - *feeling good about yourself (different from excessive pride)*

Step 1: Question
What are one or two of your greatest accomplishments?

Word Introduction: *The word **pride** means to feel good about yourself..*

Step 2: *Design*

Personified Explanation (PE): *The Design looks like the word **pride** because pride tends to grow with each and every accomplishment.*

Step 3: *Real World Association (RWA)*

In what way does the *Design* and *PE* relate to the "Real World?" Write one or more sentences relating the word **pride** to something you've learned in class, a news story, a social event, or anything you feel strongly about. Substitute the symbols in the *Design* for the real people/places/things in your *RWA*.

_____

_____

_____

Now, diagram your *RWA* using key words from the *RWA* or other words of your choice.

Step 4: Personal/Family Association (PFA)

Write one or more sentences relating the word **pride** to your own personal experience or the personal experience of someone important in your life (e.g., parent, sibling, friend). Make sure the *PFA* expresses your own or chosen others' feelings.

_____

_____

_____

Student Worksheet

Step 1: Question

Feeling Word

What are one or two of your greatest accomplishments?

Definition: _____

_____

Step 2: *Design*

Personified Explanation (PE): _____

_____

Step 3: *Real World Association (RWA)*

In what way does the *Design* and PE relate to the "Real World?" Write one or more sentences relating the word _____ to something you've learned in class, a news story, a social event, or anything you feel strongly about. Substitute the symbols in the *Design* for the real people/places/things in your *RWA*.

_____

_____

_____

Now, diagram your *RWA* using key words from the *RWA* or other words of your choice.

Step 4: *Personal/Family Association (PFA)*

Write one or more sentences relating the word _____to your own personal experience or the personal experience of someone important in your life (e.g., parent, sibling, friend). Make sure the *PFA* expresses your own or chosen others' feelings.

_____

_____

_____

Teacher Lesson Sheet

Rational - *reasonable and sensible behavior*

Step 1: Question
Why is it important to be sensible and reasonable?

Word Introduction: *To be **rational** is to be reasonable and sensible.*

Step 2: *Design*

Personified Explanation (PE): *The small lines are **rational** because they are staying away from the big lines who have a reputation of being bullies.*

Step 3: *Real World Association (RWA)*

In what way does the *Design* and *PE* relate to the "Real World?" Write one or more sentences relating the word ***rational*** to something you've learned in class, a news story, a social event, or anything you feel strongly about. Substitute the symbols in the *Design* for the real people/places/things in your *RWA*.

_____

_____

_____

Now, diagram your *RWA* using key words from the *RWA* or other words of your choice.

Step 4: Personal/Family Association (PFA)

Write one or more sentences relating the word ***rational*** to your own personal experience or the personal experience of someone important in your life (e.g., parent, sibling, friend). Make sure the *PFA* expresses your own or chosen others' feelings.

_____

_____

_____

Student Worksheet

Student name

Feeling Word

Step 1: Question
Why is it important to be sensible and reasonable?

Definition: _____

_____

Step 2: *Design*

|| ||||

Personified Explanation (PE): _____

_____

Step 3: *Real World Association (RWA)*
In what way does the *Design* and PE relate to the "Real World?" Write one or more sentences relating the word _____ to something you've learned in class, a news story, a social event, or anything you feel strongly about. Substitute the symbols in the *Design* for the real people/places/things in your *RWA.*

_____

_____

_____

Now, diagram your *RWA* using key words from the *RWA* or other words of your choice.

Step 4: *Personal/Family Association (PFA)*
Write one or more sentences relating the word _____to your own personal experience or the personal experience of someone important in your life (e.g., parent, sibling, friend). Make sure the *PFA* expresses your own or chosen others' feelings.

_____

_____

_____

Teacher Lesson Sheet

Rebellious - hard to handle

Step 1: Question
Does anyone know someone who constantly breaks the rules, does not behave, and is hard to handle?
Word Introduction: *The word **rebellious** means to be very hard to handle.*

Step 2: *Design*

Personified Explanation (PE): *The circle on the right is **rebellious** because it is not listening to the other circles who told it of the danger of crossing the line.*

Step 3: *Real World Association (RWA)*

In what way does the *Design* and *PE* relate to the "Real World?" Write one or more sentences relating the word ***rebellious*** to something you've learned in class, a news story, a social event, or anything you feel strongly about. Substitute the symbols in the *Design* for the real people/places/things in your *RWA*.

_____

_____

_____

Now, diagram your *RWA* using key words from the *RWA* or other words of your choice.

Step 4: *Personal/Family Association (PFA)*

Write one or more sentences relating the word ***rebellious*** to your own personal experience or the personal experience of someone important in your life (e.g., parent, sibling, friend). Make sure the *PFA* expresses your own or chosen others' feelings.

_____

_____

_____

Student Worksheet

Step 1: Question

Feeling Word

Does anyone know someone who constantly breaks the rules, does not behave, and is hard to handle?

Definition: _____

_____

Step 2: *Design*

Personified Explanation (PE): _____

_____

Step 3: *Real World Association (RWA)*

In what way does the *Design* and PE relate to the "Real World?" Write one or more sentences relating the word _____ to something you've learned in class, a news story, a social event, or anything you feel strongly about. Substitute the symbols in the *Design* for the real people/places/things in your *RWA*.

_____

_____

_____

Now, diagram your *RWA* using key words from the *RWA* or other words of your choice.

Step 4: *Personal/Family Association (PFA)*

Write one or more sentences relating the word _____ to your own personal experience or the personal experience of someone important in your life (e.g., parent, sibling, friend). Make sure the *PFA* expresses your own or chosen others' feelings.

_____

_____

_____

Teacher Lesson Sheet

Remorse - Regret and sorrow

Step 1: Question
What regrets do you have about something you did or did not do?

Word Introduction: *A **remorseful** person feels regret and sorrow for his or her actions.*

Step 2: *Design*

Personified Explanation (PE): *The circle feels **remorse** because it did not invite the handicapped line inside to play.*

Step 3: *Real World Association (RWA)*
In what way does the *Design* and *PE* relate to the "Real World?" Write one or more sentences relating the word ***remorse*** to something you've learned in class, a news story, a social event, or anything you feel strongly about. Substitute the symbols in the *Design* for the real people/places/things in your *RWA*.

_____

_____

_____

Now, diagram your *RWA* using key words from the *RWA* or other words of your choice.

Step 4: *Personal/Family Association (PFA)*
Write one or more sentences relating the word ***remorse*** to your own personal experience or the personal experience of someone important in your life (e.g., parent, sibling, friend). Make sure the *PFA* expresses your own or chosen others' feelings.

_____

_____

_____

Student Worksheet

Step 1: Question

Feeling Word

What regrets do you have about something you did or did not do?

Definition: _____

_____

Step 2: *Design*

Personified Explanation (PE): _____

_____

Step 3: *Real World Association (RWA)*

In what way does the *Design* and PE relate to the "Real World?" Write one or more sentences relating the word _____ to something you've learned in class, a news story, a social event, or anything you feel strongly about. Substitute the symbols in the *Design* for the real people/places/things in your *RWA*.

_____

_____

_____

Now, diagram your *RWA* using key words from the *RWA* or other words of your choice.

Step 4: *Personal/Family Association (PFA)*

Write one or more sentences relating the word _____to your own personal experience or the personal experience of someone important in your life (e.g., parent, sibling, friend). Make sure the *PFA* expresses your own or chosen others' feelings.

_____

_____

_____

Teacher Lesson Sheet

Sadism - *to gain pleasure from being cruel (distorted)*

Step 1: Question
What kind of people get pleasure from being cruel? Why do you think they act that way?
Word Introduction: *To be **sadistic** is to get pleasure from being cruel.*

Step 2: *Design*

Personified Explanation (PE): *The arrows are **sadistic** because they enjoy hurting the defenseless rectangle.*

Step 3: *Real World Association (RWA)*
In what way does the *Design* and *PE* relate to the "Real World?" Write one or more sentences relating the word ***sadistic*** to something you've learned in class, a news story, a social event, or anything you feel strongly about. Substitute the symbols in the *Design* for the real people/places/things in your *RWA*.

_____

_____

_____

Now, diagram your *RWA* using key words from the *RWA* or other words of your choice.

Step 4: Personal/Family Association (PFA)
Write one or more sentences relating the word ***sadistic*** to your own personal experience or the personal experience of someone important in your life (e.g., parent, sibling, friend). Make sure the *PFA* expresses your own or chosen others' feelings.

_____

_____

_____

Student Worksheet

Step 1: Question

Feeling Word

What kind of people get pleasure from being cruel? Why do you think they act that way?

Definition: _____

_____

Step 2: *Design*

Personified Explanation (PE): _____

_____

Step 3: *Real World Association (RWA)*

In what way does the *Design* and PE relate to the "Real World?" Write one or more sentences relating the word _____ to something you've learned in class, a news story, a social event, or anything you feel strongly about. Substitute the symbols in the *Design* for the real people/places/things in your *RWA*.

_____

_____

_____

Now, diagram your *RWA* using key words from the *RWA* or other words of your choice.

Step 4: *Personal/Family Association (PFA)*

Write one or more sentences relating the word _____to your own personal experience or the personal experience of someone important in your life (e.g., parent, sibling, friend). Make sure the *PFA* expresses your own or chosen others' feelings.

_____

_____

_____

Emotional Literacy in the Middle School   193

Teacher Lesson Sheet

Scapegoat - *being unfairly blamed for another's wrongful act*

Step 1: Question
How do you feel about people who blame others for their wrong acts?

Word Introduction: *A **scapegoat** is someone who is unfairly blamed for something he or she didn't do.*

Step 2: *Design*

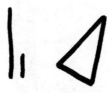

Personified Explanation (PE): *The big line knocked down the triangle and is using the small line as a **scapegoat** because it knows the small line is too frightened to say anything.*

Step 3: *Real World Association (RWA)*

In what way does the *Design* and *PE* relate to the "Real World?" Write one or more sentences relating the word ***scapegoat*** to something you've learned in class, a news story, a social event, or anything you feel strongly about. Substitute the symbols in the *Design* for the real people/places/things in your *RWA*.

_____

_____

_____

Now, diagram your *RWA* using key words from the *RWA* or other words of your choice.

Step 4: Personal/Family Association (PFA)

Write one or more sentences relating the word ***scapegoat*** to your own personal experience or the personal experience of someone important in your life (e.g., parent, sibling, friend). Make sure the *PFA* expresses your own or chosen others' feelings.

_____

_____

_____

Student Worksheet

_____
Student name

Step 1: Question

_____
Feeling Word

How do you feel about people who blame others for their wrong acts?

Definition: _____
_____

Step 2: *Design*

Personified Explanation (PE): _____
_____

Step 3: *Real World Association (RWA)*

In what way does the *Design* and PE relate to the "Real World?" Write one or more sentences relating the word _____ to something you've learned in class, a news story, a social event, or anything you feel strongly about. Substitute the symbols in the *Design* for the real people/places/things in your *RWA*.

_____

_____

Now, diagram your *RWA* using key words from the *RWA* or other words of your choice.

Step 4: *Personal/Family Association (PFA)*

Write one or more sentences relating the word _____ to your own personal experience or the personal experience of someone important in your life (e.g., parent, sibling, friend). Make sure the *PFA* expresses your own or chosen others' feelings.

_____

_____

_____

Teacher Lesson Sheet

Secure - *self-confident in your abilities*

Step 1: Question
Why is it so important to be confident in your abilities?

Word Introduction: *To be **secure** is to be self-confident and feel good about yourself and your abilities.*

Step 2: *Design*

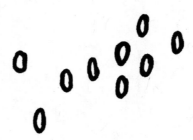

Personified Explanation (PE): *Even though the lowest circle is unable to jump as high as the other circles it is **secure** and feels that, with practice, it will be able to do so.*

Step 3: *Real World Association (RWA)*
In what way does the *Design* and *PE* relate to the "Real World?" Write one or more sentences relating the word ***secure*** to something you've learned in class, a news story, a social event, or anything you feel strongly about. Substitute the symbols in the *Design* for the real people/places/things in your *RWA*.

_____

_____

_____

Now, diagram your *RWA* using key words from the *RWA* or other words of your choice.

Step 4: *Personal/Family Association (PFA)*
Write one or more sentences relating the word ***secure*** to your own personal experience or the personal experience of someone important in your life (e.g., parent, sibling, friend). Make sure the *PFA* expresses your own or chosen others' feelings.

_____

_____

_____

Student Worksheet

Student name

Step 1: Question

Feeling Word

Why is it so important to be confident in your abilities?

Definition: _____

_____

Step 2: *Design*

0 0 0 0 0 0 0 0 0

Personified Explanation (PE): _____

_____

Step 3: *Real World Association (RWA)*

In what way does the *Design* and PE relate to the "Real World?" Write one or more sentences relating the word _____ to something you've learned in class, a news story, a social event, or anything you feel strongly about. Substitute the symbols in the *Design* for the real people/places/things in your *RWA*.

_____

_____

_____

Now, diagram your *RWA* using key words from the *RWA* or other words of your choice.

Step 4: *Personal/Family Association (PFA)*

Write one or more sentences relating the word _____to your own personal experience or the personal experience of someone important in your life (e.g., parent, sibling, friend). Make sure the *PFA* expresses your own or chosen others' feelings.

_____

_____

_____

Teacher Lesson Sheet

Self-esteem - *feeling good about yourself*

Step 1: Question
What makes people feel good about themselves?

Word Introduction: *People with **self-esteem** feel good about themselves.*

Step 2: *Design*

*Personified Explanation (PE): Because the little line has **self-esteem** it was able to convince the big lines that it is good enough to play on their team.*

Step 3: *Real World Association (RWA)*
In what way does the *Design* and *PE* relate to the "Real World?" Write one or more sentences relating the word **self-esteem** to something you've learned in class, a news story, a social event, or anything you feel strongly about. Substitute the symbols in the *Design* for the real people/places/things in your *RWA*.

_____

_____

_____

Now, diagram your *RWA* using key words from the *RWA* or other words of your choice.

Step 4: *Personal/Family Association (PFA)*
Write one or more sentences relating the word **self-esteem** to your own personal experience or the personal experience of someone important in your life (e.g., parent, sibling, friend). Make sure the *PFA* expresses your own or chosen others' feelings.

_____

_____

_____

Student Worksheet

Student name

Step 1: Question

Feeling Word

What makes people feel good about themselves?

Definition: _____

_____

Step 2: *Design*

|||||

, |||||

Personified Explanation (PE): _____

_____

Step 3: *Real World Association (RWA)*

In what way does the *Design* and PE relate to the "Real World?" Write one or more sentences relating the word _____ to something you've learned in class, a news story, a social event, or anything you feel strongly about. Substitute the symbols in the *Design* for the real people/places/things in your *RWA*.

_____

_____

_____

Now, diagram your *RWA* using key words from the *RWA* or other words of your choice.

Step 4: *Personal/Family Association (PFA)*

Write one or more sentences relating the word _____ to your own personal experience or the personal experience of someone important in your life (e.g., parent, sibling, friend). Make sure the *PFA* expresses your own or chosen others' feelings.

_____

_____

_____

Teacher Lesson Sheet

Sibling Rivalry - *conflict between sisters and brothers*

Step 1: Question
Why do you think brothers and sisters fight so much?

Word Introduction: *Sibling Rivalry is conflict between sisters and brothers.*

Step 2: *Design*

Personified Explanation (PE): *The Design looks like **sibling rivalry** because the two arrows are about to attack each other.*

Step 3: *Real World Association (RWA)*

In what way does the *Design* and *PE* relate to the "Real World?" Write one or more sentences relating the words ***sibling rivalry*** to something you've learned in class, a news story, a social event, or anything you feel strongly about. Substitute the symbols in the *Design* for the real people/places/things in your *RWA*.

_____

_____

_____

Now, diagram your *RWA* using key words from the *RWA* or other words of your choice.

Step 4: Personal/Family Association (PFA)

Write one or more sentences relating the words ***sibling rivalry*** to your own personal experience or the personal experience of someone important in your life (e.g., parent, sibling, friend). Make sure the *PFA* expresses your own or chosen others' feelings.

_____

_____

_____

Student Worksheet

Step 1: Question

Feeling Word

Why do you think brothers and sisters fight so much?

Definition: _____

_____

Step 2: *Design*

Personified Explanation (PE): _____

_____

Step 3: *Real World Association (RWA)*

In what way does the *Design* and PE relate to the "Real World?" Write one or more sentences relating the words_____ to something you've learned in class, a news story, a social event, or anything you feel strongly about. Substitute the symbols in the *Design* for the real people/places/things in your *RWA*.

_____

_____

_____

Now, diagram your *RWA* using key words from the *RWA* or other words of your choice.

Step 4: *Personal/Family Association (PFA)*

Write one or more sentences relating the words_____to your own personal experience or the personal experience of someone important in your life (e.g., parent, sibling, friend). Make sure the *PFA* expresses your own or chosen others' feelings.

_____

_____

_____

Teacher Lesson Sheet

Stress - mental or emotional strain

Step 1: Question
What kinds of things make you feel mentally strained and uptight?

Word Introduction: *To feel **stress** is to have mental or emotional strain.*

Step 2: *Design*

Personified Explanation (PE): *The dot is **stressed** because it is lost and unable to find its way out of the lines.*

Step 3: *Real World Association (RWA)*

In what way does the *Design* and *PE* relate to the "Real World?" Write one or more sentences relating the word ***stress*** to something you've learned in class, a news story, a social event, or anything you feel strongly about. Substitute the symbols in the *Design* for the real people/places/things in your *RWA*.

_____

_____

_____

Now, diagram your *RWA* using key words from the *RWA* or other words of your choice.

Step 4: *Personal/Family Association (PFA)*

Write one or more sentences relating the word ***stress*** to your own personal experience or the personal experience of someone important in your life (e.g., parent, sibling, friend). Make sure the *PFA* expresses your own or chosen others' feelings.

_____

_____

_____

Student Worksheet

Step 1: Question

Feeling Word

What kinds of things make you feel mentally strained and uptight?

Definition: _____

_____

Step 2: *Design*

Personified Explanation (PE): _____

_____

Step 3: *Real World Association (RWA)*

In what way does the *Design* and PE relate to the "Real World?" Write one or more sentences relating the word _____ to something you've learned in class, a news story, a social event, or anything you feel strongly about. Substitute the symbols in the *Design* for the real people/places/things in your *RWA*.

_____

_____

_____

Now, diagram your *RWA* using key words from the *RWA* or other words of your choice.

Step 4: *Personal/Family Association (PFA)*

Write one or more sentences relating the word _____ to your own personal experience or the personal experience of someone important in your life (e.g., parent, sibling, friend). Make sure the *PFA* expresses your own or chosen others' feelings.

_____

_____

_____

Teacher Lesson Sheet

Terror - *Overpowering fear*

Step 1: Question
What is one of your greatest fears?

Word Introduction: *To feel **terror** is to experience overpowering fear.*

Step 2: *Design*

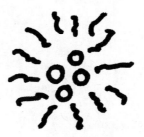

Personified Explanation (PE): *The circles are **terrorized** by the sudden appearance of strange and unusual squiggles around them.*

Step 3: *Real World Association (RWA)*
In what way does the *Design* and *PE* relate to the "Real World?" Write one or more sentences relating the word ***terror*** to something you've learned in class, a news story, a social event, or anything you feel strongly about. Substitute the symbols in the *Design* for the real people/places/things in your *RWA*.

_____

_____

_____

Now, diagram your *RWA* using key words from the *RWA* or other words of your choice.

Step 4: *Personal/Family Association (PFA)*
Write one or more sentences relating the word ***terror*** to your own personal experience or the personal experience of someone important in your life (e.g., parent, sibling, friend). Make sure the *PFA* expresses your own or chosen others' feelings.

_____

_____

_____

Student Worksheet

_____
Student name

Step 1: Question

_____
Feeling Word

What is one of your greatest fears?

Definition: _____

_____

Step 2: *Design*

Personified Explanation (PE): _____

_____

Step 3: *Real World Association (RWA)*
In what way does the *Design* and PE relate to the "Real World?" Write one or more sentences relating the word _____ to something you've learned in class, a news story, a social event, or anything you feel strongly about. Substitute the symbols in the *Design* for the real people/places/things in your *RWA*.

_____

_____

_____

Now, diagram your *RWA* using key words from the *RWA* or other words of your choice.

Step 4: *Personal/Family Association (PFA)*
Write one or more sentences relating the word _____ to your own personal experience or the personal experience of someone important in your life (e.g., parent, sibling, friend). Make sure the *PFA* expresses your own or chosen others' feelings.

_____

_____

_____

Teacher Lesson Sheet

Unique - one of a kind, different

Step 1: Question
What do you regard as special and different about yourself?

Word Introduction: *To be **unique** is to be one of a kind and different.*

Step 2: *Design*

Personified Explanation (PE): *All of the shapes are **unique** because they each have a distinct appearance.*

Step 3: *Real World Association (RWA)*

In what way does the *Design* and *PE* relate to the "Real World?" Write one or more sentences relating the word ***unique*** to something you've learned in class, a news story, a social event, or anything you feel strongly about. Substitute the symbols in the *Design* for the real people/places/things in your *RWA*.

_____

_____

_____

Now, diagram your *RWA* using key words from the *RWA* or other words of your choice.

Step 4: *Personal/Family Association (PFA)*

Write one or more sentences relating the word ***unique*** to your own personal experience or the personal experience of someone important in your life (e.g., parent, sibling, friend). Make sure the *PFA* expresses your own or chosen others' feelings.

_____

_____

_____

Student Worksheet

Feeling Word

Step 1: Question

What do you regard as special and different about yourself?

Definition: _____

_____

Step 2: *Design*

Personified Explanation (PE): _____

_____

Step 3: *Real World Association (RWA)*
In what way does the *Design* and PE relate to the "Real World?" Write one or more sentences relating the word _____ to something you've learned in class, a news story, a social event, or anything you feel strongly about. Substitute the symbols in the *Design* for the real people/places/things in your *RWA*.

_____

_____

Now, diagram your *RWA* using key words from the *RWA* or other words of your choice.

Step 4: *Personal/Family Association (PFA)*
Write one or more sentences relating the word _____to your own personal experience or the personal experience of someone important in your life (e.g., parent, sibling, friend). Make sure the *PFA* expresses your own or chosen others' feelings.

_____

_____

Appendices

A. Alphabetized list of 63 Feeling Words
B. Word-Pairs for Creative Writing Assignments
C. Introducing Regular Vocabulary Words
D. Sample Family Letter

Appendix A
Alphabetized List of 63 Feeling Words
(Use of alternate forms of each word should be encouraged) e.g., adapt, adaptation; addiction, addicted

- Adapt
- Addiction
- Agony
- Alienation
- Altruism
- Ambivalent
- Anxiety
- Apprehension
- Arrogant
- Attitude
- Commitment
- Communicate
- Compassion
- Compromise
- Cope
- Depression
- Deprivation
- Despair
- Devastated
- Discouraged
- Elation
- Empathy
- Enraged
- Enthusiasm
- Envious
- Exhilaration
- Externalize
- Forlorn
- Frustration
- Greedy
- Guilty
- Hostile

- Humble
- Identify
- Impulsive
- Indivisible
- Inhibition
- Insecure
- Internalize
- Intimate
- Irrational
- Jubilant
- Loathe
- Loyalty
- Masochistic
- Motivation
- Obsession
- Optimism
- Patience
- Pessimism
- Prejudice
- Pride
- Rational
- Rebellious
- Remorse
- Sadistic
- Scapegoat
- Secure
- Self-esteem
- Sibling Rivalry
- Stress
- Terror
- Unique

Appendix B
Word-Pairs for Creative Writing Assignment

Word-pairs consist of sophisticated synonyms (e.g., pride and pleasure) and antonyms (e.g., sibling rivalry and delight). These require students to synthesize definitions of the words and to apply them creatively in an essay.

1. sad → adapt
2. happy → addiction
3. agony → content
4. sad → altruism
5. cheerful → ambivalent
6. anxiety → joy
7. confident → apprehension
8. arrogant → sad
9. angry → attitude
10. lonely → communicate
11. funny → compassion
12. hate → compromise
13. depressed → cope
14. depression → hopeful
15. deprivation → content
16. despair → hatred
17. devastated → accustomed
18. discouraged → hopeful
19. jealous → empathy
20. enraged → sorry
21. enthusiasm → shyness
22. envious → secure
23. scared → exhilaration
24. externalized → confident
25. forlorn → happy
26. frustration → enjoyed
27. greedy → nervous
28. guilty → relaxed
29. hostile → lonely
30. humble → happy
31. angry → identify
32. impulsive → fearful
33. indivisible → strong
34. inhibition → confident
35. insecure → sorry
36. internalize → quiet
37. intimate → happy
38. irrational → confused
39. scared → jubilant
40. loathe → selfish
41. uncertain → loyalty
42. masochistic → sad
43. tired → motivation
44. obsession → panic
45. optimism → excited
46. annoyed → patience
47. pessimism → surprised
48. prejudice → sad
49. pride → delight
50. nervous → rational
51. content → rebellious
52. mean → remorse
53. sadistic → fearful
54. scapegoat → shame
55. panic → secure
56. unhappy → self-esteem
57. sibling-rivalry → delight
58. stress → thankful
59. terror → anxiety
60. unique → appreciated

Appendix C
Introducing Traditional Words

Questions used to introduce traditional vocabulary words are very similar to the questions provided in this program. They help students link the idea or meaning of the new word to personal experiences. Remember, a good question helps students relate to the new word both intellectually and emotionally.

When constructing a question for a traditional vocabulary word, the teacher should first think of the meaning of the word and then what word or words relate to the chosen word. For example, the word allegiance might conjure up words like friendship, loyalty, country, etc. These key words will trigger a personal experience, idea, or situation, which acts as a basis for the question. Since traditional vocabulary words are not "emotionally" charged, the questions should be constructed to elicit opinions and reactions from the students. Below are four examples.

Allegiance – faithfulness
(Brings up the idea of friendship)
Possible Questions: "What is important in a close relationship or marriage?" "What do you regard as important in a good friendship?" "What do you feel you owe your country?"
Anecdotes/Discussion...
Introduction: What we are talking about is being faithful to someone or something. There is a word that describes these thoughts and feelings. The word is allegiance.

Civic duty – a citizen's responsibility
(brings up idea of contributing to society)
Possible Questions: "What are some duties or responsibilities a citizen has to his town, state, and nation?" "It's not what your country can do for you, it's what you can do for your country. What does this statement mean?"
Anecdotes/Discussion...
Introduction: The things or duties we have been discussing are called civic duties.

Example 2: Historical Reference
Question: "In Ancient Greece, citizens were fined if they didn't live up to specific kinds of responsibilities such as voting. Do you think you or your parents should be penalized for not voting?"
Anecdotes/Discussion...
Introduction: Well, whether or not you are in favor of penalties for not voting - voting itself is an important responsibility of citizens in all democratic nations. It is one of the responsibilities or duties that is referred to as a civic duty.

Agora – a meeting place in Ancient Greece

(brings up idea of people getting together)

Possible Questions: "Where do you usually get together to hang out in town?"

Anecdotes/Discussion...

Introduction: You all have a lot in common with the citizens in ancient Greece, as they too had a meeting place. It was a market place called an <u>Agora</u>.

Oligarchy - 4 people of equal power who ruled the Roman Empire

(brings up thoughts and feelings of having more than 1 boss to report to)

Possible Questions: "How would you feel if there were three or four presidents of the United States; or if there were three or four captains on your baseball team?"

Anecdotes/Discussion...

Introduction: "In ancient Rome, at the beginning of Julius Caesar's reign, the Roman Government was ruled by four people of equal power, two tribunes who represented the poor and two consuls who represented the rich. This ancient Roman government is referred to as the <u>Roman Oligarchy</u>.

It is critical to stay within this given sequence when introducing words:

(1) Ask a prepared question to the class.

(2) Wait for student (or teacher) anecdote(s).

(3) Introduce the new word. This sequence helps ensure that the meaning of the word has been assimilated. Then students are assigned to write three sentences for homework.

Homework assignment for traditional vocabulary words:

1. Write the word with its definition in sentence form:
   Example: The word <u>allegiance</u> means to be faithful.
2. Write one or more sentence(s) relating the word to something you've learned in class, a news report, or a social situation (local, national or international):
   Example: The <u>allegiance</u> between the allies in WWII was a major reason for the victory. (History)
3. Write one or more sentence(s) using the word to describe a personal experience, reaction, or opinion:
   Example: For me, the most precious thing in a good friendship is <u>allegiance</u>.

Appendix D
Sample Family Letter

Dear Parent/Guardian/Family Members:

As part of our general literacy studies, students are learning strategies to enable them to more accurately and confidently represent their thoughts and feelings. The program focuses on the development of an "emotions vocabulary", reading comprehension, and oral and written expression.

Part of this program requires students to make a connection between new *feeling* words, which are part of the emotions vocabulary, and real-world social and personal experiences. Additionally students are to work with family members to relate these words to their own personal experiences or those of the family members. This requires the help of a family member to assist the child in relating an assigned *feeling* word to a personal experience that the family member or child has had. An example of a personal experience using the *feeling* word *alienated* might be, "I don't play baseball very well and sometimes that makes me feel *alienated* from my friends." As your child will have a choice whether or not to share their personal experience with the class, we ask that all topics be appropriate for class discussion. The child or family member will also be asked to use a *feeling* word to relate to a real-world social experience. Using the same word *alienated,* an example of this might be, "China and the USA are *alienated* from each other because of different political and economic beliefs."

Thank you for your time and contribution to your child's academic and social development.

Yours truly,

References

Achenbach, T., & Howell, C. (1994). Are America's children's problems getting worse? A 13-year comparison. *Journal of the American Academy of Child and Adolescent Psychiatry, 32,* 1145-1154

Brackett, M. A., & Mayer, J. D. (2003). Convergent, discriminent, and incremental validity of competing measures of emotional intelligence. *Personality and Social Psychology Bulletin, 29,* 1147-1158.

Brackett, M. A., Mayer, J. D., & Warner, R. M. (2004). Emotional intelligence and its expression in everyday behavior, *Personality and Individual Differences, 36,* 1387-1402.

Brenner, B., & Salovey, P. (1997). Emotion regulation during childhood: Developmental, interpersonal, and individual considerations. In P. Salovey, & D. Sluyter (Eds.), *Emotional development and emotional intelligence.* New York: Basic Books.

Caine, R. & Caine, G. (1994). *Making connections: Teaching and the human brain.* Menlo park, CA: Addison-Wesley.

Ciarrochi, J. V., Chan, A. Y. C., & Caputi, P. (2000). A critical evaluation of the emotional intelligence construct. *Personality and Individual Differences, 28,* 539-561.

Clott, J. (1998, September). Bottom of the class. *Rutgers Magazine,* 5-7.

Daiute, C. & Buteau, E. (2002). Writing for Their Lives: Children's Narrative Supports for Physical and Psychological Well-Being. In Lepore, S.J. & Smyth, J.M. (Eds.), *The Writing Cure: How Expressive Writing Promotes Health and Emotional Well-Being.* Washington, D.C.: American Psychological Association, 53-75.

Damásio, A. R. (1994). *Descartes' error: Emotion, reason, and the human brain.* New York: Putnam.

Danish, S. (1997). Going for the goal: A life skills program for adolescents. In G. Albee, & T. Gullotta. *Primary prevention's works. (Vol. 6). Issues in children's and families lives.* (p. 291). New York: Sage.

Davidson, R., & Cacioppo, J. (1992). New developments in the scientific study of emotion: An introduction to the special section. *Psychological Science, 3,* 21-22.

Dryfoos, J. G. (1997). The prevalence of problem behaviors: Implications for programs. In R. P. Weissberg, T. P. Gullotta, R. L. Hampton, B. A. Ryan, & G. R. Adams (Eds.), *Healthy children 2010: Enhancing children's wellness* (pp. 17-46). Thousand Oaks, CA: Sage.

Eisenberg, N., Fabes, R. A., Guthrie, I. K., & Reiser, M. (2000). Dispositional emotionality and regulation: Their role in predicting quality of social functioning. *Journal of Personality and Social Psychology, 78,* 136-157.

Eisenberg, N., Fabes, R., Murphy, B., Maszk, P., Smith, M. & Karbon, M. (1995). The role of emotionality and regulation in children's social functioning: A longitudinal study. *Child Development, 66,* 1360–1384.

Elias, M., Zins, J., Weissberg, R., Frey, K., Greenberg, T., Haynes, N., Kessler, R., Schwab-Stone, M., & Shriver, T. (1997). *Promoting social and emotional learning: Guidelines for educators.* Alexandria, VA: Association for Supervision and Curriculum Development.

Estimation methodology for children with a serious emotional disturbance. *Federal Register.* (1997, October 6). pp. 52139-52144.

Feldman, R. S., Philippot, P., & Custrini, R. J. (1991). Social competence and nonverbal behavior. In R. S. Feldman & B. Rime (Eds.), *Fundamentals of nonverbal behavior* (pp. 329-350). New York: Cambridge University Press.

Gardner, H. (1983/1993). *Frames of mind: The theory of multiple intelligences.* New York: Basic Books.

Goleman, D. (1995*). Emotional Intelligence.* New York: Bantam Books.

Gottfredson, D.D., & Gottfredson, G. D. (2002). Quality of school-based prevention programs: Results from a national survey. *Journal of Research in Crime and Delinquency, 39,* 3-35.

Gottman, J. (2001). Meta-emotion, children's emotional intelligence, and buffering children from marital conflict. In C. D. Ryff & B. H. Singer (Eds.), *Emotion, social relationships, and health.* New York: Oxford University Press.

Greenberg, M. T., Weissberg, R. P. O'Brien, M. U., Zins, J., Fredericks, L., Resnik, H., & Elias, M. J. (2003). Enhancing school-based prevention and youth development through coordinated social, emotional, and academic learning. [Peer Reviewed Journal] *American Psychologist, 58,* 466-474.

Gullotta, T. (1990). Preface. In T. Gullotta, G. Adams, & R. Montemayor (Eds.). *Developing social competency in adolescence.* (pp. 7-8). Newbury Park, CA: Sage.

Halberstadt, A. G., Denham, S. A., & Dunsmore, J. C. (2001). Affective social competence. *Social Development, 10,* 79-119.

Hamburg, D.A. (1992). *Today's children: Creating a future for a generation in crisis.* New York: Times Books.

Hawkins, J. D., Catalano, R. F., Kosterman, R., Abbott, R., & Hill, K. G. (1999). Preventing adolescent health-risk behaviors by strengthening protection during childhood. *Archives of Pediatric & Adolescent Medicine, 153,* 226-334.

Jacobs, W. & Nadel, L. (1985). Stress-induced recovery of fear and phobias. *Psychological Review, 92,* 512-531.

Kantrowitz, B. and Wingert. P. (1999, May 10). Beyond Littleton: How well do you know your kid? *Newsweek,* 36-39.

Lloyd, A. C. (1978). Emotion and decision in stoic psychology. In J. M. Rist (Ed). *The Stoics (pp. 233-246).* Los Angeles, CA: University of California Press.

Lopes, P. N., & Salovey, P. (2004). Toward a broader education: Social, emotional, and practical skills. In J. E. Zins, R. P. Weissberg, and H. Walberg (Eds.), *Social and Emotional Learning and School Success.* New York: Teachers College Press.

Lopes, P. N., Brackett, M. A., Nezlek, J. B., Schutz, A., Sellin, I, & Salovey, P. (in press). Emotional intelligence and social interaction. *Personality and Social Psychology Bulletin.*

Martin, S. (1998, October). Seligman laments people's tendency to blame others. *APA Monitor,* 50.

Mayer, J. D., & Salovey, P. (1997). What is emotional intelligence? In P. Salovey & D. Sluyter (Eds.), *Emotional development and emotional intelligence: Implications for educators* (pp. 3-31). New York: Basic Books.

Mayer, J. D., Caruso, D. R., & Salovey, P. (1999). Emotional intelligence meets traditional standards for an intelligence. *Intelligence, 27,* 267-298.

Nellum-Williams, R. (1998). Educator's commentary. (p. 164). In P. Salovey, & D. Sluyter. (1997). *Emotional development and emotional intelligence.* New York: Basic Books.

Orlich, D., Harder, R., Callahan, R., & Gibson, H. (1998). *Teaching strategies.* (p. 213-214). New York: Houghton Mifflin Company.

Palfai, T. P., & Salovey, P. (1993). The influence of depressed and elated mood on deductive and inductive reasoning. *Imagination, Cognition, and Personality, 13,* 55-71.

Payton, J. W., Graczyk, P. A., Wardlaw, D. M., Bloodworth, M., Tompsett, C. J., & Weissberg, R. P. (2000). Social and emotional learning: A framework for promoting mental health and reducing risk behavior in children and youth. *Journal of School Health, 70,* 179-185.

Pennebaker, J. W. (1997). Writing about emotional experiences as a therapeutic process. *Psychological Science, 8,* 162-166.

Plutchik, R.(1984). Emotions: A general psychoevolutionary theory. In K. R. Scherer and P. Ekman. (Eds). *Approaches to Emotion,* 197-219. Hillsdale, NJ: Erlbaum.

Rubin, M. M. (1999). *Emotional intelligence and its role in mitigating aggression: A correlational study of the relationship between emotional intelligence and aggression in urban adolescents.* Unpublished Dissertation, Immaculata College, Immaculata, Pennsylvania.

Saarni, C. (1999). *The development of emotional competence.* New York: The Guilford Press.

Salovey, P., & Mayer, J. D. (1990). Emotional intelligence. *Imagination, Cognition, and Personality, 9,* 185-211.

Salovey, P., & Sluyter, D. J. (Eds.). (1997). *Emotional development and emotional intelligence: Educational implications.* New York: Basic Books.

Schoenberg, P. (1981, April 3). Monticello students examine accused assassin's catalysts. *Middletown Times Herald Record,* p. 8.

Sylwester, R. (Ed.). (1998). *Student brains, school issues: A collection of articles.* Arlington Heights, IL: SkyLight.

Sylwester, R. (1995*). A celebration of neurons: An educator's guide to the human brain.* Alexandra, VA: Association for Supervision and Curriculum Development.

Takanishi, R. (1993, February). The opportunities of adolescence. *American Psychologist, 48,* 85-87

Trinidad, D. R., & Johnson, C. A. (2001). The association between emotional intelligence and early adolescent tobacco and alcohol use. *Personality and Individual Differences, 32,* 95-105.

Trinidad, D. R., Unger, J. B., Chou, C. P., & Johnson, C.A. (in press). The protective association of emotional intelligence with psychosocial smoking risk factors for adolescents. *Personality and Individual Differences.*

Vogel, G. (1997, February 28). Scientist probe feelings behind decision-making. *Science, 275*, 1269.

Weissberg, R. P, & Greenberg, M. (1998). School and community competence-enhancement and prevention programs. In W. Damon (Series Ed.) & I. E. Siegel & K. A. Renninger (Vol. Eds.), *Handbook of social psychology: Vol. 4. Child psychology in practice* (5the ed., pp. 877-954). New York: Wiley.

Weissberg, R., Barton, H., & Shriver, T. (1996). The social-competence promotion program for young adolescents. In G.W. Albee & T.P. Gullotta (Eds.). *Primary prevention exemplars: The Lela Rowland Awards.* (p. 270). Newbury Park, CA: Sage Publications.

Zins, J. E., Elias, M. J., Greenberg, M. T., & Weissberg, R. P. (2000). Promoting social and emotional competence in children. In K. M. Minke & G. C. Bear (Eds.), *Preventing school problems — promoting school success: Strategies and programs that work* (pp. 71-99). Washington, DC: National Association of School Psychologists.

Resources
Available from National Professional Resources, Inc.
(Print & Video)
1-800-453-7461/www.NPRinc.com

Armstrong, Thomas. *7 Kinds of Smart: Identifying and Developing Your Many Intelligences, Revised*. New York, NY: Plume (The Penguin Group), 1999.

Armstrong, Thomas. *Multiple Intelligences: Discovering the Giftedness in All* (Video). Port Chester, NY: National Professional Resources, Inc., 1997.

Beane, Allan L. The Bully Free Classroom: *Over 100 Tips and Strategies for Teachers K-8*. Minneapolis, MN: Free Spirit Publishing, 1999.

Bocchino, Rob. *Emotional Literacy: To be a Different Kind of Smart*. Thousand Oaks, CA: Corwin Press, 1999.

Casbarro, Joseph. *Test Anxiety & What You Can Do About It*. Port Chester, NY: National Professional Resources, Inc. 2003.

Cohen, Jonathan (editor). *Educating Hearts and Minds: Social Emotional Learning and the Passage into Adolescence*. New York, NY: Teachers College Press, 1999.

Coles, Robert. *Moral Intelligence of Children*. New York, NY: Random House, Inc., 1997.

De Klerk, Rina, & le Roux, Ronel. *Emotional Intelligence for Children & Teens: A Practical Guide For Parents and Teachers*. Port Chester, NY: National Professional Resources, Inc., In press.

De Klerk, Rina, & le Roux, Ronel. *Emotional Intelligence Workbook: The All-In-One Guide for Optimal Personal Growth*. Port Chester, NY: National Professional Resources, Inc., In press.

DeRoche, Edward F. & Williams, Mary M. *Educating Hearts & Minds*. Thousand Oaks, CA: Corwin Press, 1998.

Elias, Maurice, et al. *Engaging the Resistant Child Through Computers: A Manual to Facilitate Social and Emotional Learning*. Port Chester, NY: National Professional Resources, Inc., 2001.

Elias, Maurice, et al. *EQ & IQ = Best Leadership Practices for Caring and Successful Schools*. Thousand Oaks, CA: Corwin Press, 2002.

Elias, Maurice. *Raising Emotionally Intelligent Teenagers: Parenting with Love, Laughter and Limits.* New York, NY: Three Rivers Press, 1999.

Elias, Maurice, et al. *Promoting Social-Emotional Learning: Guidelines for Educators.* Alexandria, VA: ASCD, 1997.

Elias, Maurice, & Tobias, Steven. *Social Problem Solving: Interventions in the Schools.* New York, NY: Guilford Press, 1996.

Etzioni, Amit. *New Golden Rule: Community & Morality.* New York, NY: Basic Books, 1996.

Feldman-Barrett, L., & Salovey, P. (Eds.). *The Wisdom in Feeling:Psychological Processes in Emotional Intelligence.* New York, NY: Guilford Press, 2002.

Gardner, Howard. *Frames of Mind: The Theory of Multiple Intelligences* (10th Anniversary Edition). New York, NY: Basic Books, 1993.

Gardner, Howard. *How Are Kids Smart? Multiple Intelligences in the Classroom* (Video). Port Chester, NY: National Professional Resources, Inc., 1995.

Gardner, Howard. *The Unschooled Mind: How Children Think and How Schools Should Teach.* New York, NY: Basic Books, 1991.

Glasser, William. *Choice Theory: A New Psychology of Personal Freedom.* New York, NY: HarperCollins, 1998.

Goleman, Daniel. *Emotional Intelligence: A New Vision for Educators* (Video). Port Chester, NY: National Professional Resources, Inc., 1996.

Goleman, Daniel. *Emotional Intelligence: Why it Matters More Than IQ.* New York, NY: Bantam Books, 1995.

Jensen, Eric. *Successful Applications of Brain-Based Learning* (Two video set). Port Chester, NY: National Professional Resources, Inc., 2000.

Jensen, Eric. *Tools for Engagement: Managing Emotional States for Learner Success.* San Diego, CA: The Brain Store, 2003.

Josephson, Michael & & Hanson, Wes. *Power of Character: Prominent Americans Talk About Life, Family, Work, Values & More.* San Francisco, CA: Jossey-Bass, 1998.

Kagan, Spencer. *Building Character Through Cooperative Learning* (Video). National Professional Resources, Inc., 1999.

Krovetz, Martin L. *Fostering Resiliency: Expecting All Students to Use Their Minds and Hearts Well.* Thousand Oaks, CA: Corwin Press, 1999.

LeDoux, Joseph. *The Emotional Brain.* New York, NY: Simon & Schuster, 1996.

Levine, Mel. *A Mind at a Time.* New York, NY: Simon & Schuster, 2002.

Levine, Mel. *Developing Minds Multimedia Library (Videos).* Boston, MA: WGBH, 2001.

Lickona, Thomas et al. *Character Education: Restoring Respect & Responsibility in Our Schools* (Video). National Professional Resources, Inc., 1996.

Lickona, Thomas. *Character Matters.* Carmichael, CA: Touchstone Books, 2004.

Lickona, Thomas. *Educating for Character: How our Schools can Teach Respect & Responsibility.* New York, NY: Bantam Books, 1992.

Lickona, Thomas. *Raising Good Children.* New York, NY: Bantam Books, 1994.

Macan, Lynn, et al. *Character Education: Application in the Classroom, Elementary Edition* (Video). National Professional Resources, Inc., 1998.

Mayer, J.D., Salovey, P. and Caruso, D. *Emotional intelligence as Zeitgeist, as personality, and as a mental ability.* In R. Bar-On and J.D.A. Parker (Eds.) *The Handbook of Emotional Intelligence* (pp. 92-117). San Francisco, CA: Jossey-Bass, 2000.

Mayer, J.D., Salovey, P. and Caruso, D. *Models of emotional intelligence.* In R.J. Sternberg (Ed.), *The Handbook of Intelligence* (pp.396-420). New York, NY: Cambridge University Press, 2000.

Mayer, J.D., Caruso, D. and Salovey, P. *Selecting a measure of emotional intelligence: The case for ability scales.* In R. Bar-On and J.D.A. Parker (Eds.) *The Handbook of Emotional Intelligence* (pp.320-342). San Francisco, CA: Jossey-Bass, 2000.

Mayer, J.D., Salovey, P. and Caruso, D. *The Mayer-Salovey-Caruso Emotional Intelligence Test (MSCEIT).* Toronto, ON: MultiHealth Systems, 2001.

Pert, Candace. *Emotion: Gatekeeper to Performance* (Video). Port Chester, NY: National Professional Resources, Inc., 1999.

Pert, Candace. *Molecules of Emotion.* New York, NY: Scribner, 1997.

Salovey, P., & Sluyter, D. (Eds.). *Emotional Development and Emotional Intelligence: Implications for Educators.* New York, NY: Basic Books, 1997.

Salovey, P., et al. *Emotional Intelligence: Key Readings on the Mayer and Salovey Model.* Port Chester, NY: National Professional Resources, Inc., 2004.

Salovey, Peter et al. *Optimizing Intelligences: Thinking, Emotion & Creativity* (Video). National Professional Resources, Inc., 1998.

Sergiovanni, Thomas J. *Moral Leadership: Getting to the Heart of School Improvement.* San Francisco, CA: Jossey-Bass, 1992.

Shelton, Claudia M. & Stern, Robin. *Understanding Emotions in the Classroom: Differentiating Teaching Strategies for Optimal Learning.* Port Chester, NY: National Professional Resources, Inc., 2004.

Shore, Kenneth. *ABC's of Bullying Prevention.* Port Chester, NY: National Professional Resources, Inc., 2004.

Stirling, Diane, Archibald, Georgia, McKay, Linda & Berg, Shelley. *Character Education Connections for School, Home and Community.* Port Chester, NY: National Professional Resources, Inc., 2002.

Teele, Sue. *Rainbows of Intelligence: Exploring How Students Learn.* Thousand Oaks, CA: Corwin Press, 1999.

Teele, Sue. *Rainbows of Intelligence: Raising Student Performance Through Multiple Intelligences* (Video). Port Chester, NY: National Professional Resources, Inc., 2000.

Wolfe, Patricia. *Brain Matters: Translating Research into Classroom Practice.* Alexandria, VA: ASCD, 2001.

Videos available from National Professional Resources, Inc.

Optimizing Intelligences:
Thinking, Emotion & Creativity

Video

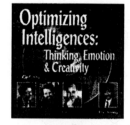

CD-ROM

<u>**Video:**</u> This exciting video, hosted by *Peter Salovey* and featuring *Mihaly Csikszentmihalyi, Howard Gardner,* and *Daniel Goleman,* will expand your knowledge by explaining the **three theories that are revolutionizing our thinking about intelligence, emotion, and creativity.** These psychologists challenge many of our traditionally held beliefs about learning and intelligence. Their views are making a great impact in our schools, mental health facilities and even in our work place. Learn the valuable applications of these theories in your classrooms.

VHS, 45 minutes
Order #VOPI-BRAC (Closed Captioned)   **$99.95**
Also available with Spanish subtitles
Order # VOPS-BRAC   **$109.95**

<u>**CD-ROM:**</u> National Professional Resources, Inc. converts its best-selling video to CD-ROM. This interactive format makes it easy to learn more about the three theories that are revolutionizing our thinking about intelligence, emotion and creativity. Learning is more effective when it is interactive. This combination of text, video and resources is an ideal medium to obtain a better understanding of the research and learn about the valuable applications of their theories in schools and mental health settings. PC & Mac compatible

2002, CD-ROM   **Order # OICD-BRAC**   **$89.95**

How Are Kids Smart?
Multiple Intelligences in the Classroom
Howard Gardner

Learn about MI theory, and observe first hand how teachers have incorporated MI theory into their teaching, classrooms and community. No longer do we ask "How smart are our kids?" but "How are kids smart?" A must for every classroom teacher struggling with the challenges of increasing diversity, inclusion of students with special needs and the move toward heterogeneous grouping. A note to Special Educators: Observe a student with disabilities in an MI program and the parent's perspective.

VHS, 31 minutes   **Order #VMIT-BRAC**   **$69.00**
Spanish subtitled version   **Order # VKST-BRAC**   **$79.00**

Educating for Understanding
by Project Zero
at Harvard Graduate School of Education

This comprehensive professional development program, filmed at Harvard University, presents the work of **Project Zero**, a research group at the **Graduate School of Education** that explores the development of learning in children, adults, and organizations. Through this video series and accompanying staff development guide, **Project Zero** staff provide an examination of how <u>understanding</u> can be viewed, taught, assessed, and deepened. Former co-directors of Harvard's Project Zero, **Howard Gardner** and **David Perkins**, present a foundation upon which the concept of <u>understanding</u> can be more fully explored, evaluated and enhanced. Presenting with **Drs. Gardner and Perkins** in this video series are many senior researchers from **Project Zero**, who are internationally renowned in the field of teaching and learning, and provide a complete package for teachers, administrators, professors, and staff developers who are committed to improving <u>understanding</u> in all environments, and for learners of all ages. The accompanying **staff development guide** provides valuable suggestions for the most effective use of the videos. Glossaries of terms as well as additional resources are included.

THE SERIES INCLUDES EIGHT VIDEOTAPES
AND A PROFESSIONAL DEVELOPMENT GUIDE

Tape #	Presenter
1. Experiencing Understanding	Tina Blythe
2. Unmasking Understanding	David Perkins
3. Minds and Understanding	Howard Gardner
4. The Teaching for Understanding Framework	Lois Hetland, Tina Blythe, Mark Church, Shehla Ghouse, & Joan Soble
5. Understanding in the Disciplines	Veronica Boix Mansilla
6. The Mindful Classroom	Ron Ritchhart
7. Rubrics for Thinking and Understanding	Heidi Goodrich Andrade
8. Collaborative Assessment	Steve Seidel

Set Includes:
Eight Videos (35 to 85 minutes each), and One Guide to the Video Series. PRICE:$895 Order #VPRZE-BRAC (additional Guides may be purchased for $19.95; Order # PRZEG-BRAC)

Emotional Intelligence:
A New Vision for Educators

Presented by Daniel Goleman

Drawing on groundbreaking research, Goleman shows that Emotional Intelligence is more important than IQ. Research indicates that our emotions play a much greater role in decision-making and individual success than has been commonly acknowledged. Join Dan Goleman and educators as they effectively implement Emotional Intelligence.   **VHS, 40 minutes**

Order # VEIN-BRAC   **$89.95**
Also available with Spanish subtitles
Order # VEIS-BRAC   **$99.95**

About the Authors

Marvin Maurer, M.A.

Emotional Literacy in the Middle School was originally conceptualized and created as the "Little People Feeling Words Curriculum" in the early 70's by Mr. Maurer, who began his career as a middle school Social Studies, English and Math teacher in upstate New York. Throughout the last 30 years, Mr. Maurer has implemented programs pertaining to the role of emotions and their importance in the learning process. In addition, as a presenter for the New York State Department of Education, he championed the need for affective education with traditional curriculum. Mr. Maurer also designed the first gifted program for the Monticello, NY school system and has worked as a learning disabilities consultant within the school system and as a private practitioner. Mr. Maurer currently teaches for universities and colleges in the state of Florida and maintains a private practice of clients with whom he uses the strategies of *Emotional Literacy in the Middle School.*

Marc A. Brackett, Ph.D.

Marc Brackett is Associate Director of the Health, Emotions, and Behavior Laboratory and Lecturer in the Department of Psychology at Yale University. He received his doctorate from the University of New Hampshire, where he studied under Dr. Jack Mayer, co-founder of the Emotional Intelligence theory. Dr. Brackett's first line of research focuses on emotion intelligence and how the construct relates to social competence, broadly defined (e.g., interpersonal relationships, drug use, and social deviance). He has also developed a theoretical model and measurement tool of the Life Space, which organizes a person's external surroundings to provide extensive external criteria to test associations between internal personality characteristics and people's behavior. Dr. Brackett regularly teaches introductory and personality psychology at Yale and works with school systems and corporations in the areas of assessment, training, and leadership development. He also holds a 5th degree black belt in Hapkido, a Korean martial art.

Francesca, Plain, Ed.D.

Francesca Plain holds a doctorate in Educational Leadership and a master's degree in Learning Disabilities. She currently serves as a Learning Consultant for the West Morris Regional High School District in Chester, New Jersey. Her expertise includes the areas of special education, staff and curriculum development. Dr. Plain has a well-rounded educational background having held positions as a director of special education, and elementary and middle school administrator. She has written extensively on inclusion and teacher assessment, presented at state and national conferences, and created a video on homework practices. Dr. Plain is also president of Eduscapes Consulting Services, a northern New Jersey based educational consulting company. In addition, she enjoys teaching special education courses at William Paterson University in Wayne, New Jersey. Dr. Plain is the educational consultant for Emotional Literacy in the Middle School.

The authors are available for training and/or in-service staff development on this program. Contact Marc Brackett at emotionliteracy@aol.com, or at 203-432-2332.